THE GIFT OF NOT KNOWING

HOW LETTING GO OPENS THE WAY TO DEEPER FAITH

THE GIFT OF NOT KNOWING
BOOK 1

PASTOR JOSE R. PEREZ

PASTOR JOSE R. PEREZ MINISTRIES

COPYRIGHT

DEDICATION

This book is dedicated to those who were raised in God's name but never knew His heart.

To the children who learned fear before love, performance before presence, and silence before safety.

To the sons who lost hope under the weight of expectations they could never fulfill.

To the daughters who were shamed instead of protected, controlled instead of covered, and blamed for wounds they never chose.

To those who walked away from Christ—not because they rejected Him, but because they were never truly allowed to know Him.

To those whose pain was dismissed as rebellion, whose questions were treated as threats, and whose suffering was spiritualized instead of healed. And to those we lost, whose despair ran deeper than the answers they were given:

This book is written with the hope that you will discover that God was never the one who wounded you, and that truth—when finally freed from fear—does not crush the soul; it restores it.

WITH GRATITUDE
TO OUR SUPPORTERS

This book was made possible through the encouragement and generosity of friends and family who believed in this message and supported its development and publication.

With sincere appreciation, I acknowledge the following individuals whose partnership helped bring *The Gift of Not Knowing* to life:

Supporters

Carlos C. Perez

Candy and Joseph Carlson

Dr. Benjamin Grajales

Marcos Naranjo

Judge Luis G. Perez

Rev. Aaron R. Payson

Ruben Burgos

Your encouragement and belief in this message are deeply appreciated.

May this work bless others, just as you have blessed this project.

Pastor Jose R. Perez

CONTENTS

INTRODUCTION

When More Knowledge Isn't the Answer

Most people believe that clarity comes from knowing more. We assume that if we gather enough information, study harder, pray longer, and accumulate spiritual insight, we will finally understand what God is doing.

But Scripture presents a different reality: clarity does not come from knowing more—it comes from revelation.

Human sight is limited. Human perception is shaped by wounds, culture, emotion, environment, and spiritual atmosphere. Human reasoning can only interpret what the senses provide, and most of life's deepest realities do not exist in the realm of the senses at all.

We chase answers, but God offers something better: spiritual sight. We chase explanations, but God offers discernment. We chase information, but God offers revelation.

This is the turning point at the center of this book: you don't need to know more—you need to see differently.

Book One introduced this truth—that God hides certain things not to punish us, but to protect us, shape us, and draw us deeper into trust. Book Two goes further. It shows what happens when you stop trying to master knowledge and begin to live by revelation.

This book will take you through the limits of human knowledge, the formation of perception, the reality of the unseen realms, and the lifestyle of walking in revelation.

You will learn why the senses can mislead, why culture shapes beliefs without permission, why atmospheres matter, why spiritual warfare begins with perception, and why God uses time, seasons, and mystery to guide us into maturity.

Then, in the final movement of this book, you will learn how to hear God clearly, discern truth from deception, renew your mind, walk in spiritual authority, and live a life shaped by revelation, not reaction.

This is not a book about accumulating facts. It is a book about transformation. Revelation must become obedience. Insight must become lifestyle. Truth must become the rhythm of your daily choices.

The Gift of Not Knowing is not about ignorance—it is about dependence. It teaches you to navigate life not with perfect understanding, but with perfect trust.

My prayer is that as you turn these pages, your spiritual eyes will open, your perception will sharpen, your heart will quiet, and your discernment will deepen. And you will begin to walk in the light God has already given you.

Because the greatest gift God can give is not the answer to every question, but the revelation that leads you to His heart.

PART I

THE LIMITS OF HUMAN KNOWLEDGE

1

THE GIFT OF NOT KNOWING

Section 1: Why God Limits What We See

God did not create our limits by accident. Our understanding is limited. Our perception remains partial. Our ability to see the full picture is restrained. These limits are not punishment; they are protection. Human beings were not designed to carry unlimited knowledge. We were designed to live in trust.

When God formed Adam from the dust, He gave him life—not omniscience. He placed him in a garden, gave him instructions, and walked with him. Adam was not created to function through self-sufficient knowledge, but through relationship.

It is common to think that knowing more would make life easier —that answers would calm fear and clarity would provide control. But from the beginning, Scripture reveals something different. Knowledge, when separated from God, does not bring life; it leads to destruction. It was not ignorance that broke the world. It was knowledge pursued apart from Him.

We often think of God's protection in physical terms—danger avoided, harm prevented. Yet one of His greatest protections is what He chooses not to reveal.

If you knew every betrayal before it happened, could you still love freely? If you saw every storm before it formed, would you still walk in peace? If your entire future were visible, would faith have any room to grow?

We pursue foresight. God is forming trust.

So He withholds—not to frustrate us, but to preserve what we are not yet ready to carry. Too much knowledge, too soon, would distort us. Fear would paralyze us. Pride would quietly take root.

God leads differently—not through full explanations, but through relationship, one step at a time. Scripture says we walk by faith, not by sight (2 Corinthians 5:7). Sight has value, but it was never meant to lead.

Human perception is limited and easily misread. You can see clearly with your eyes and still miss what God is doing. You can understand your circumstances and still misunderstand Him. Faith carries us where knowledge cannot.

God does not give the whole map. He gives the next step.

As long as we trust ourselves more than Him, we will resist that process. But not knowing forces something we often avoid—it creates dependence. And dependence is where relationship with God lives.

Some of the things we ask God to show us would overwhelm us. We pray for clarity, for understanding, for full revelation. But if those prayers were fully answered, we would not be strengthened—we would be crushed.

Jesus told His disciples, "You cannot bear them now" (John 16:12). Not because they could not understand, but because they could not carry it. God reveals according to capacity, not curiosity.

Some truths require maturity before they make sense, healing before they bring freedom, and growth before they bring stability. Not knowing is not a delay; it is preparation.

Trust only exists where certainty is absent. If everything were visible, trust would not be required. If every outcome were clear, faith would not be necessary.

The unknown keeps us close to God. It draws us into prayer. It teaches us to listen. It prevents self-sufficiency.

We were not created to carry certainty. We were created to carry His presence.

And His presence is enough.

Section 2: Knowledge Without God Becomes a Trap

To understand the danger of knowledge, we must return to the moment humanity first reached for it. The serpent did not ask for worship. He offered something far more subtle—independence: "You will be like God..." (Genesis 3:5).

The temptation was never about fruit. It was about autonomy—the ability to define good and evil apart from God.

The moment Adam and Eve accepted that idea, something shifted—not because knowledge increased, but because trust moved. The relationship between God and humanity fractured—not on the basis of what was known, but on who was trusted. That foundation has never changed.

When Eve took the fruit, she did not gain clarity. She gained knowledge her spirit was not prepared to carry. Nothing outward collapsed in that moment, but everything within began to shift. The conscience became unstable. Perception lost its steadiness. Emotions no longer aligned. Reasoning became inconsistent.

Before the fall, humanity saw through God's truth. After the fall, humanity began seeing through its wounds.

The issue has never been knowledge itself. It is knowledge separated from God. Without Him, knowledge does not lead to understanding—it leads to distortion.

That same pattern continues today. It no longer appears in the same form, but the invitation remains unchanged: "Follow your heart." "Live your truth." "Do what feels right." Different language—but the same direction: become your own authority.

Once truth is defined apart from God, its foundation shifts. What was once anchored becomes unstable.

Today, we live in a world saturated with information. It is constant, immediate, and unending. But information without God does not produce wisdom. It produces instability.

The more voices shape perception without discernment, the

easier it becomes to drift. Confidence turns into pride. Understanding gives way to confusion. Questions multiply into doubt. Possibilities expand into fear. Slowly—and often unnoticed—self-reliance replaces dependence.

The issue is not access to knowledge. It is the absence of guidance.

When Adam and Eve ate from the tree, humanity did not gain wisdom. It gained wounds. Nothing visibly collapsed, yet internally everything fractured. Innocence gave way to shame. Confidence was replaced with self-consciousness. Relationship with God was disrupted. Identity became uncertain.

Knowledge without God does not strengthen the soul. It burdens it. It produces fear, control, and a quiet need to manage what was never meant to be carried alone.

Faith becomes performance. Identity becomes fragile. Life becomes something to hold together instead of something received.

Scripture warns, "Lean not on your own understanding" (Proverbs 3:5). Not because human understanding has no value, but because it was never meant to lead.

Reality is often interpreted through emotion, experience, culture, fear, and desire. When knowledge is filtered through what is broken, it becomes unreliable. This is why timing is misread, why God's voice is misunderstood, and why His silence can feel confusing instead of intentional.

The mind was never designed to lead. It was designed to follow.

Scripture also says, "The fear of the Lord is the beginning of wisdom" (Proverbs 9:10). Wisdom does not begin with understanding. It begins with surrender.

Knowledge seeks answers. Wisdom follows God—even without them.

In a world overflowing with information, the need is not more knowledge. It is guidance.

God is not looking for people who understand everything. He is looking for people who trust Him in anything.

Because the most dangerous knowledge is not what you don't know—it is what you assume you know without God.

Section 3: Faith Lives Where Answers Are Incomplete

There is a reason God did not give Adam and Eve a complete understanding from the beginning. They were not created to operate from full knowledge. They were created to walk with Him. Human beings were designed for dependence, not self-sufficiency—for relationship, not autonomy. Our strength has never been in what we know, but in who we follow.

This is why Scripture says, "The righteous shall live by faith" (Romans 1:17). Faith exists where something remains unknown. If everything were visible, it would have no place to grow. If everything made sense, trust would not be required.

So God leaves space—where understanding ends and relationship begins.

Throughout Scripture, God rarely reveals the full plan. He gives direction, but not full explanation—a word, a step, a promise, but not the outcome. Noah was told to build, but not how long he would wait. Abraham was told to go, but not where he was going. Moses was told to act, but not how the sea would respond. The disciples were told to cross, but not about the storm ahead.

Why?

Because faith requires God to lead—and us to follow.

If everything were revealed, dependence would fade. Trust would weaken. Faith does not grow through complete explanation. It grows when what is visible cannot explain what is happening.

In those moments, something deeper forms. Prayer becomes intentional. Attention sharpens. Awareness of need increases. Faith does not grow when life is controlled. It grows when life is uncertain and trust remains.

Those who walked closely with God were not the ones who understood everything. They were the ones who continued to follow without needing to.

Faith is not the absence of questions. Some of the deepest moments of faith in Scripture came through them: "How long, O

Lord?" "Why have You forsaken Me?" Questions, when brought to God, do not weaken faith; they deepen it.

Faith is not proven by having answers. It is revealed by remaining with God without them.

Looking back, the greatest growth rarely comes through clarity. It comes through uncertainty. In seasons where direction is unclear, answers are delayed, and outcomes are hidden, something deeper is being formed.

What appears unclear is not empty. It is active.

Not knowing does not mean nothing is happening. It means something is being shaped beneath the surface.

The desire for certainty is natural. The desire for control is strong. We want understanding before we move. But faith does not operate that way. It requires surrender. It calls for movement without full clarity—trusting not in what is seen, but in who God is.

Faith is not about knowing the plan. It is about trusting the One who holds it.

You are not called to understand everything. You are called to follow Him through anything.

And when His hand cannot be traced, His character becomes the anchor.

That is faith. That is maturity. That is the gift of not knowing.

2

THE BOUNDARIES OF GOD'S REVELATION

Section 1: God Reveals What We Need, Not Everything We Want

One of the hardest truths to accept is that God does not tell us everything. Not because He withholds what is good, but because He understands what the human heart can carry. Revelation is intentional. Silence is purposeful. Even mystery carries purpose.

Spiritual maturity begins when we recognize the difference between what we want to know and what God knows we are ready to receive.

From Genesis to Revelation, God never gives unlimited access to knowledge. Even the angels have limits (Matthew 24:36). That alone reveals something essential: knowledge is not the highest goal. Revelation is not the end. Relationship is.

God does not measure maturity by what is known, but by how a person responds to what has already been revealed.

The pattern throughout Scripture is consistent: enough light is given for the next step while the rest remains hidden to preserve dependence. If everything were revealed at once, the tendency would be to move ahead without Him.

So God leads differently—not with full explanations, but with sufficient direction. Not with complete clarity, but with enough light to obey.

Revelation is aligned with capacity. God does not reveal simply to inform. He reveals to transform. Every true revelation carries purpose. It directs, corrects, forms, and moves life forward—not just understanding.

If what is received does not lead to change, it remains information rather than revelation.

This is why Jesus said, "To you it has been given..." (Matthew 13:11). Revelation is not earned. It is entrusted—and entrusted where there is alignment with what has already been given.

Scripture says, "The secret things belong to the Lord..." (Deuteronomy 29:29). Some things God keeps hidden—not because He is distant, but because He is protective.

The desire for full understanding is natural. We want details, outcomes, explanations. Yet some things remain unrevealed—timing still forming, outcomes still unfolding, reasons not yet clear.

This is not absence. It is preparation.

If certain truths were revealed too early, they would overwhelm rather than strengthen. Misunderstanding would distort them. Pain could deepen instead of heal. So God shields what cannot yet be carried.

Silence is not abandonment. Hiddenness is not rejection. It is an invitation to trust.

It is often assumed that seeking more will automatically result in receiving more. But revelation is not given through desire alone. It is entrusted where there is capacity.

Clarity does not increase where surrender is absent. Insight does not deepen where obedience is resisted. What is revealed is connected to what is followed.

Revelation carries responsibility. It is not given to satisfy curiosity, but to deepen relationship.

God is not revealing things to impress. He is revealing things to transform.

The desire to know everything is not neutral. It reflects the same impulse that seeks independence from God.

The serpent's strategy was not simply deception—it was suggestion: God is holding something back from you.

That pattern remains. It appears in thoughts like: "You need more answers before you can trust Him." "You cannot move forward until everything makes sense."

But trust is not built on information. It is built on who God is.

God maintains a tension we often resist: enough light to move forward, but not enough to remove the need for Him. There is always enough to obey, enough to follow, enough to pray, enough to trust—but never enough to become independent.

This is not limitation. It is mercy.

Space remains within understanding so that closeness to His voice is not lost.

You do not need to know everything. You need to trust the One who does.

This is where maturity begins. This is where relationship deepens. This is the gift of not knowing.

Section 2: Why Some Truths Remain Hidden

There is a dimension of God that will always remain beyond human understanding. Some things are revealed. Others are withheld. Scripture does not soften this reality: "The secret things belong to the Lord our God..." (Deuteronomy 29:29).

There are truths we receive, truths we grow into, and truths we may never fully understand in this life. This is not a failure of faith—it is part of God's nature and His protection.

Not all knowledge strengthens. Some of it overwhelms. Some reshapes perception in ways that do not bring clarity. Knowledge is not neutral. It can burden, distort, and destabilize.

So when God withholds, He is not depriving—He is guarding.

There are realities that, if revealed too early or too fully, would weigh more than the heart can carry. They would confuse rather than clarify and weaken faith rather than strengthen it. So God establishes a boundary—not to distance Himself, but to protect.

Silence is often misunderstood. When God does not explain, it can feel like distance. When He does not make known, it can feel like something is missing.

But silence is not absence. It is restraint.

What feels like distance may actually be protection.

God does not always remove uncertainty. He often uses it. Strength forms in that tension. Maturity develops in waiting. Endurance is shaped in what remains unresolved.

Mystery is not a barrier. It is a place of formation.

In a world that pursues deeper knowledge—hidden meanings, spiritual insight, and what feels significant—it is easy to lose sight of purpose. Revelation is not given to satisfy curiosity. It is given to strengthen obedience.

When revelation is collected rather than followed, it loses its purpose. What was meant to draw a person closer to God can quietly become something that elevates them instead.

That shift matters.

Revelation without obedience leads to pride. And pride creates distance.

God does not reveal to impress. He reveals to shape.

The questions carried through life are often real: Why did this happen? Why wasn't it stopped? Why does God not explain?

At times, God does not answer with information. He answers with Himself. Explanation cannot restore the soul. His presence can. Understanding does not always bring peace. His nearness does.

Some things may never be fully understood. Yet it is still possible to be held.

Scripture draws a clear boundary. Some things belong to God. Some things belong to us.

What belongs to Him remains in His hands—His timing, His purposes, His reasons, His unseen work.

What belongs to us is simpler, but no less important: obedience, faith, trust, surrender.

Confusion begins when we try to carry what was never given.

When we reach for what God has kept hidden, we repeat the same pattern—seeking knowledge outside of trust.

Maturity begins when the question changes—not "Why hasn't God told me?" but "Can I trust Him even when He doesn't?"

That shift changes everything. It anchors faith. It moves the focus from needing answers to knowing Him.

You do not need to understand everything. You need to trust the One who does.

Section 3: Revelation Draws Us Into Relationship

God does not reveal Himself to make us smarter. He reveals Himself to draw us closer. Revelation is not information. It is invitation. It draws attention, leads the heart, and creates nearness—not through force, but through clarity.

Every true revelation is relational at its core.

Before God revealed doctrine, law, or prophecy, He revealed Himself through presence. Adam did not learn about God through instruction alone. He learned by walking with Him. God did not begin with explanation. He began with fellowship.

That has not changed.

He still reveals Himself through nearness—through His voice, through quiet clarity, through an awareness that cannot always be explained, but can be recognized. To the hungry, He draws near. To the broken, He meets gently. To the surrendered, He reveals more deeply.

Revelation does not simply give knowledge about God. It brings a person into relationship with Him.

This is why knowledge without relationship becomes dangerous. The Pharisees knew the Scriptures—but not the One who spoke them. Jesus said, "You search the Scriptures... yet you refuse to come to Me" (John 5:39–40). They knew the text, but not the Author.

That difference is critical.

Knowledge without relationship leads to pride. Insight without surrender leads to self-reliance. What begins as understanding can quietly create distance. It produces the appearance of closeness without the reality of it.

When God reveals something, He is not simply teaching—He is drawing. When Scripture comes alive, it is not only information—it is His heart being made known. When something within is exposed, it is not for shame, but for healing. When direction becomes clear, it is not a map being handed over—it is an invitation to walk with Him.

Revelation always leads to deeper dependence. If it does not change the way you walk with God, it remains information.

Jesus said, "Blessed are the pure in heart, for they shall see God" (Matthew 5:8). Revelation is not given according to intellect. It is given according to posture. A humble heart hears differently. A surrendered life sees more clearly. Dependence creates awareness that others overlook.

God reveals Himself to those who draw near—not to those who only seek to understand.

Revelation also carries responsibility. It can soften the heart or harden it—depending on the response. Every moment of revelation becomes a crossroads: response or resistance.

What God reveals is not meant to remain in the mind. It is meant to shape how life is lived.

At its core, revelation has one purpose: relationship.

Everything returns to this.

God reveals because He desires nearness—not performance, not understanding alone, but relationship. He reveals to draw close. He withholds to build trust. He speaks to create connection. He remains silent at times to deepen pursuit.

If revelation becomes anything other than relationship, the focus has shifted.

Jesus said, "My sheep hear My voice... and they follow Me" (John 10:27). Revelation is not measured by how much is understood. It is recognized by His voice.

When Scripture comes alive—it is His voice. When conviction rises—it is His voice. When clarity forms in prayer—it is His voice. When direction becomes steady—it is His voice.

The purpose of revelation is not depth. It is relationship.

Everything God makes known is meant to draw you closer—closer to His voice and closer to His heart.

3

WHY GOD HID THE TREE

Section I: The Purpose Behind the Forbidden Knowledge
To understand the fall, a deeper question must be asked: Why did God forbid the tree in the first place?

God does not restrict without purpose. He does not withhold out of insecurity. He does not limit knowledge to keep humanity small. Whenever God hides something, it is for protection.

The tree was not forbidden because it was evil. It was forbidden because humanity was not created to carry what it contained.

The greatest threat was never the serpent itself. It was independence from God.

When the serpent said, "You will be like God..." (Genesis 3:5), the offer was not about fruit. It was about autonomy—the ability to define truth, identity, and morality apart from Him.

That is what the tree represented: life outside of dependence.

Humanity was created to live differently—to walk with God, depend on His voice, and receive truth from His presence. But when knowledge is separated from God, it does not produce wisdom. It produces distortion.

The tree was not simply about knowledge. It involved a kind of awareness humanity was not prepared to bear. To "know good and evil" was not just intellectual. It was experiential—it meant carrying the weight of moral conflict, shame, fear, guilt, and inner tension.

There was no framework for that. The mind was unburdened. The heart was unscarred. Identity was secure.

Introducing that level of awareness would not elevate—it would overwhelm.

God did not restrict the tree because He lacked trust. He restricted it because capacity had not yet been formed.

Before the fall, humanity was led by God. Afterward, it began to follow its own understanding. That shift changed everything.

Human beings were never created to navigate life through intellect alone, self-analysis, or independent reasoning. They were created to be led.

Once knowledge replaces dependence, confusion follows.

Without God, knowledge does not steady the soul—it unsettles it. It produces pride, fear, overthinking, and a gradual drift into self-reliance.

The serpent understood this. The goal was not simply disobedience. It was self-sufficiency.

Innocence is often misunderstood. It is not ignorance. It is uncorrupted perception. Humanity lived in trust, peace, clarity, and relationship.

That innocence was not weakness. It was protection.

God guarded it because innocence allows a person to live without the internal weight of fear, shame, and conflict.

Once that innocence was lost, everything changed—not around them first, but within them.

God understood something humanity did not: some knowledge does not simply inform—it reshapes from within.

To "know" evil is not to study it. It is to experience its effect.

Humanity was not designed to carry that weight apart from Him.

So God withheld the tree—not to limit, but to protect.

Because human capacity has limits. Because knowledge carries weight. Because independence leads to separation.

The tree was never about restriction. It was about protection.

Humanity reached for knowledge it was not meant to carry—and stepped outside the relationship it was created to live in.

Everything that follows begins there.

Section 2: Knowledge Humanity Was Not Meant to Carry

In forbidding the Tree of the Knowledge of Good and Evil, God was not withholding wisdom. Adam and Eve already had access to truth. They walked with God. They heard His voice.

What was withheld was not information, but a kind of awareness humanity was never designed to carry.

The awareness offered in the garden was not intellectual. It was experiential. To "know" good and evil was not simply to understand it. It was to feel it, carry it, and be shaped by it from within.

It introduced something entirely new into the human experience: shame, fear, guilt, and internal conflict.

This kind of awareness does not remain external. It reshapes from within.

The human soul was never designed to carry that weight apart from God.

The serpent's promise made this clear: "You will be like God..." (Genesis 3:5). This was not about gaining insight. It was about gaining self-rule—the ability to define truth, identity, and morality apart from God.

Once that shift occurs, stability begins to erode. Truth becomes something interpreted instead of received. Identity becomes something constructed instead of given. What once felt certain becomes negotiable.

This is not wisdom. It is separation from the source of truth.

The knowledge of evil is not neutral. It cannot be held at a distance. To "know" evil is to become aware of something that alters perception. Fear surfaces. Anxiety takes root. Internal tension forms.

Humanity was not created to interpret life through that lens. Life was meant to be lived in clarity, peace, trust, and direct relationship with God.

But the tree introduced a reality humanity was never meant to inhabit.

One of the deepest consequences of this awareness is awareness without resolution. After the fall, humanity became aware of sin, but had no power over it. It became sensitive to guilt, but had no way to be cleansed. It could recognize what was broken, but could not restore it.

The conscience awakened. But the covering was gone.

No human being can carry that weight alone.

God was already forming humanity through relationship. Growth was meant to unfold over time—through obedience, trust, and walking with Him.

But the serpent offered something different: a shortcut. Instant awareness without process. Insight without formation.

What is gained quickly, without formation through relationship, rarely remains stable.

True growth transforms. Shortcut knowledge bypasses that transformation and leaves a person carrying what they were never prepared to hold.

At its core, this awareness appealed to something deeper: pride—the desire to function without God, the belief that truth can be determined independently.

That impulse has not disappeared. It still surfaces in subtle ways—in the assumption that understanding is enough, that direction can be determined without Him, that dependence is optional.

But the moment self-sufficiency takes hold, alignment is lost.

The knowledge itself was never the problem. The problem was carrying it without God.

Humanity reached for something it was never designed to hold—and took on a weight it could not sustain.

That is the nature of forbidden knowledge.

Section 3: The Cost of Forbidden Knowledge

There are two tragedies in the story of the fall. The first is that Adam and Eve ate from the tree. The second is what that act awakened within them.

Forbidden knowledge rarely feels dangerous at first. It feels like insight, clarity, something gained. But it always carries a cost. By the time that cost becomes visible, it is already unfolding.

Adam and Eve believed they were gaining something. In reality, they lost far more than they received.

Before the fall, trust in God was simple. His voice was clear. His presence was natural. His goodness was unquestioned.

But the moment doubt entered—even before the fruit was taken—something began to shift. The suggestion that God might be withholding something planted suspicion. Once trust weakens, relationship no longer feels effortless. What once felt natural now requires restoration.

After the fall, obedience no longer flowed from the heart in the same way. It began to feel optional. The desire to decide apart from God started to grow. What once felt like freedom in relationship began to feel like limitation.

Independence appears empowering at first—but it leads elsewhere. The moment we become our own authority, we also become responsible for what we were never created to sustain.

Before the fall, there was no internal conflict—no tension between desire and obedience, no struggle between truth and impulse.

Afterward, something divided within humanity. Awareness of what is right remained, but the ability to consistently live it out did not. That tension was never part of God's design. It was introduced when humanity took on knowledge it was not meant to carry alone.

Something else shifted as well. Before the fall, awareness was centered on God. Afterward, it turned inward. Attention moved toward vulnerability, insecurity, and constant self-evaluation.

With that shift came a weight the human soul was never meant to carry. As life becomes centered on self, anxiety follows—because the soul was not designed to sustain that level of internal focus.

The serpent promised clarity. What humanity received was distortion. Nothing in creation changed, but the way it was perceived did. Trust gave way to suspicion. Peace was replaced by fear. Confidence turned into shame.

The greatest damage was not external. It was internal. The way reality was interpreted had been altered.

Before the fall, God's voice guided everything. Afterward, it became one voice among many. Fear, guilt, desire, and confusion began to compete for attention. Internal noise increased. Clarity faded.

Life apart from God became disoriented—because the human soul was never meant to carry that many competing influences.

And perhaps the greatest cost was this: humanity became aware of evil, but lost the ability to overcome it. Sensitivity to sin increased, but the strength to resist it did not. What was wrong could be recognized, but what was right could not be consistently lived.

That is the weight of forbidden knowledge. It exposes, but does not restore. It reveals, but does not redeem.

The fall was not an increase in understanding. It was a loss of alignment. Humanity reached for knowledge it was never designed to carry—and stepped into a condition it could not repair.

That is the cost of forbidden knowledge.

4

THEIR EYES WERE OPENED

Section I: What Really Happened in Eden

Everything changed in a single moment. Not when the serpent spoke. Not when the fruit was considered. But when humanity received a kind of knowledge it was never designed to carry.

Scripture captures it simply: "Then the eyes of both of them were opened..." (Genesis 3:7). But what opened was not clarity. It was a new way of seeing—shaped by separation rather than by God.

They did not gain vision. They lost innocence.

Before the fall, awareness was centered on God. His presence was known. His voice was recognized. The world was experienced as He defined it.

Afterward, that awareness turned inward. The focus shifted. What had once been anchored in relationship became centered on self. For the first time, humanity became its own reference point.

That shift may seem small. But it changed everything.

The human soul was never designed to carry that weight.

Before the fall, there was no fear. Nothing was interpreted as threat. But once perception changed, experience followed. Adam said, "I was afraid..." (Genesis 3:10). Fear did not come from circumstance. It came from separation. It emerges when life is interpreted without the covering of His presence.

Something else entered as well. What had once felt natural now felt exposed. Shame is more than embarrassment. It is a shift in identity—a quiet sense that something is wrong at the core.

Before the fall, there was no hiding, no self-judgment, no comparison. Afterward, they covered themselves. They no longer saw themselves through God's design, but through a distorted lens.

Once that distortion took hold, it began to affect everything. Nothing in creation had changed, but the way it was interpreted had.

Previously, innocence shaped understanding. Now fear began to guide interpretation.

The serpent promised enlightenment. What humanity received was distortion.

That distortion still echoes—in how people are misread, how situations are misjudged, and how even God is misunderstood.

The issue is not what is seen. It is how it is seen.

Before the fall, there was no internal conflict. Desire and obedience moved in the same direction.

Afterward, something divided within humanity. Awareness of good and evil came, but without the power to live it out consistently. With that awareness came tension. What is right can be recognized, yet not consistently lived.

That tension was never part of God's design. It began in Eden.

The final shift was relational. Scripture says, "They hid themselves from the presence of the Lord..." (Genesis 3:8). God had not moved. But their perception of Him had.

What once brought joy now stirred fear. What once drew them close now caused them to withdraw.

Sin did not remove God's presence. It changed how it was experienced.

So the opening of their eyes was not a gain. It was a loss.

It marked the beginning of fear, shame, distortion, inner conflict, and separation.

Humanity began to see—but without the clarity that comes from God.

And that condition still shapes every human life today.

Section 2: The Birth of Shame, Fear, Hiding, and Separation

As Scripture states, their eyes were opened, marking the beginning of a new human condition. Humanity stepped out of innocence and into an internal reality it was never created to carry.

What followed was immediate and unmistakable—not learned behaviors, but conditions that began shaping the human soul from that moment forward: shame, fear, hiding, separation.

These are not merely reactions. They are patterns that continue to shape human life.

The first shift was internal. Adam and Eve no longer saw themselves the same way. What once felt natural now felt exposed, and what had been secure now felt unstable. Something in their sense of identity had changed.

Shame goes deeper than guilt. Guilt speaks to what is done. Shame reshapes who a person believes they are. It distorts identity, weakens confidence, and disrupts intimacy.

From that moment forward, humanity no longer stood before God with simplicity. Self-awareness now carried weight.

Fear followed. "I was afraid..." (Genesis 3:10). Before the fall, there was no anticipation of harm. Nothing was interpreted as threat.

Once that covering was lost, uncertainty entered.

Fear is more than an emotion. It arises when life is interpreted without the assurance of God's presence. It creates an expectation of loss, exposure, and rejection—even when those things are not present.

What began in Eden did not remain confined there. It continues to echo within the human heart.

Shame and fear do not remain isolated. They lead somewhere.

"They hid themselves..." (Genesis 3:8).

Hiding was not about location. It was about withdrawal. Adam and Eve stepped back because they no longer believed they could remain exposed before God. Something within them felt unsafe being seen.

That instinct remains.

Hiding becomes the attempt to protect what feels broken. It appears in different forms—avoidance, performance, distraction—but the root is the same: the fear of being fully known.

From there, separation took hold—not because God moved away, but because humanity did. What once felt natural in relationship now felt strained. What once drew them near now caused them to withdraw.

God's presence had not changed. But their ability to remain in it had.

Separation is not always visible, but it is deeply felt. It appears as distance in prayer, loss of clarity, and confusion about who God is and how He sees us.

It is the condition of a heart trying to approach God while carrying something it was never meant to hold alone.

These four—shame, fear, hiding, and separation—are not isolated. They are connected. Each leads to the next, forming a pattern that continues to shape life outside of innocence.

This is the condition that began in Eden.

And apart from God, it continues to repeat.

Section 3: How the Fall Still Shapes Human Perception

As Adam and Eve's eyes were opened, the change went far deeper than a moment of emotion. It altered how humanity interprets reality. Physical sight did not change. Inner perception did.

The inner lens through which life is understood—self, others, and God—was reshaped. And that change did not remain in Eden. What began there still shapes how life is seen today.

Before the fall, trust was natural. Afterward, fear took its place. Life began to be interpreted through uncertainty and self-protection rather than confidence in God.

That shift continues to influence decisions, relationships, and faith. Where trust once led, fear now competes.

Identity was also affected. Instead of receiving identity from God, humanity began defining it internally. This introduced instability. Awareness of self increased, but certainty of identity decreased.

This is where insecurity begins, where comparison takes root, and where self-judgment becomes familiar.

Shame no longer remains an experience. It becomes a lens.

And once identity is filtered through that lens, stability is lost.

The fall also altered how people see one another. In place of clarity, there is now misinterpretation. Suspicion replaces trust. Defensiveness replaces openness.

Relationships begin to require effort—not because they were designed that way, but because perception is no longer whole. What was meant to be natural now requires restoration.

The most significant distortion, however, is how humanity sees God. After the fall, Adam withdrew—not because God had changed, but because perception had.

That same distortion remains.

God may be acknowledged, yet His character is questioned. His intentions are misunderstood. His silence is misread. His presence is often interpreted through fear instead of confidence.

The issue is not God's distance. It is how He is seen.

Within the human heart, another tension continues. The fall introduced a divided inner life. There is a desire for what is right, yet a struggle to choose it. A longing for closeness, yet resistance to vulnerability.

This is more than internal conflict. It reflects a fractured condition.

At its core, the fall disrupted how humanity sees itself. Before, identity was received. After, it became something to secure.

So identity is pursued through achievement, approval, and comparison—attempting to define what was never meant to be constructed.

But none of these restore what was lost.

Identity was never meant to be built. It was meant to be received from God.

So the opening of human eyes did not produce clarity. It produced distortion.

That distortion still shapes how life is seen—how we understand ourselves, how we interpret others, how we approach God, and how we move through the world.

This is why restoration is not only about forgiveness. It is about seeing clearly again.

5

THE BIRTH OF SHAME, FEAR, AND SELF-CONSCIOUSNESS

Section 1: Shame as a Barrier to God

Shame was the first wound to enter the human heart. It was not learned over time. It did not come through culture, trauma, or experience. It appeared the moment humanity received knowledge it was never meant to carry.

Before that moment, life was marked by innocence—fully known, unafraid, and secure in God's presence. Identity was not questioned. Worth was not earned. Relationship with God was natural.

Then something shifted.

Awareness turned inward. Self-consciousness replaced innocence.

Shame alters how a person sees themselves. What once felt natural now feels exposed, and what once felt secure now feels uncertain.

But shame does more than point to failure. It reshapes identity. Guilt says, I did something wrong. Shame says, Something is wrong with me.

That shift is what makes shame destructive. It moves from behavior to identity—from action to worth.

Before the fall, Adam and Eve moved toward God without hesitation. Afterward, they withdrew. Nothing about God had changed. But everything about how they saw Him—and themselves—had.

Shame creates distance. It convinces us we are unworthy of God's presence, that we must fix ourselves before we approach Him, and that it is safer to hide than to be seen.

Once that belief takes hold, relationship no longer feels natural. It becomes strained.

Their first response was to cover themselves. They sewed fig leaves together—not because it restored anything, but because it felt necessary.

That instinct remains.

People still attempt to cover what they fear will be rejected—through performance, achievement, image, and even religious activity. But self-made coverings do not heal the soul. They only hide what needs to be restored.

As God called out, "Where are you?" (Genesis 3:9), He was not seeking information. He was initiating restoration.

Shame moves us away from God. But God moves toward us.

He does not expose to condemn. He draws near to restore.

The question was never about location. It was about relationship. Where has shame led you? Why are you hiding?

This is still how God meets us.

Shame did not originate in God. It entered through separation. It fills the space where connection has been lost—keeping people from prayer, silencing worship, and convincing them they are unworthy.

But shame's voice is not the final authority.

After the fall, God clothed Adam and Eve—not with something they created, but with something He provided.

That moment reveals a lasting truth: what shame exposes, only God can cover. Human effort cannot restore identity. Only God can.

Even here, the story points forward—to a covering that would not be temporary, but complete.

Shame tells us to stay away. God invites us to come near.

Shame says hide. God calls us forward.

Shame insists that repair must come first. God receives us as we are—and restores us Himself.

The answer to shame is not concealment. It is returning to the One who restores what was lost.

Section 2: Fear Distorts Our Perception

Fear entered the human experience the moment humanity stepped out of God's covering. It was never part of creation. It was never something the human soul was designed to carry.

Adam's first recorded words after the fall reveal the shift: "I was afraid..." (Genesis 3:10).

Fear was not simply an emotion. It became a condition. From that moment forward, it began shaping how reality is interpreted.

Before the fall, there was security—no anticipation of danger, no need for self-protection. Afterward, nothing in the environment changed, but the way it was interpreted did.

Fear reshapes perception. What is unknown feels threatening. What is uncertain feels dangerous. The future feels unstable.

This is what happens when life is viewed without awareness of God's presence.

The distortion does not stop with circumstances. It reaches into how God is seen. The same God who once brought joy now stirred fear—not because He changed, but because perception did.

Fear reshapes how He is understood. A Father can feel distant. A refuge can seem uncertain. A source of life can become something quietly avoided.

Many still live in that tension—believing in God, yet struggling to trust His character.

Fear interprets Him through distance instead of relationship.

But Scripture reminds us, "Perfect love casts out fear" (1 John 4:18). Fear is not removed through effort. It is displaced when God's love becomes real again.

Fear also reshapes how we see ourselves. Confidence gives way to insecurity. Certainty is replaced with doubt.

A different voice begins to speak—subtle, persistent, and familiar: You are not enough. You cannot handle this. You are alone.

Over time, that voice begins to shape identity. Instead of seeing ourselves through God's design, we begin interpreting ourselves through limitation.

Fear narrows the soul. It leads to hesitation, silence, and withdrawal.

It also affects how others are seen. Where trust once had room to grow, suspicion takes root. Rejection is anticipated. Harm is expected —even when nothing has happened.

This is why relationships feel more difficult than they should. Fear creates distance. It shifts the focus from understanding to self-protection.

Fear does not remain internal. It shapes action. As God calls forward, fear introduces hesitation. It makes obedience feel heavier than it is.

Where God says move, fear suggests delay. Where God says trust, fear raises doubt. Over time, it keeps people from stepping into what God is asking.

At its core, fear imagines a future without God. It projects outcomes where He does not provide, does not speak, and does not intervene.

This is why Scripture calls us not to fear—not because challenges are absent, but because God is present.

Fear distorts reality. Faith restores it.

Fear is not removed by reasoning. It quiets as God's presence becomes real again.

When He draws near, stability returns. What once felt overwhelming becomes steady. What once felt uncertain becomes anchored.

Fear loses its influence when God is seen clearly again.

Section 3: Self-Consciousness Replaces God-Consciousness

One of the most significant shifts in the fall was not only what humanity felt, but where its focus moved.

Before sin, attention was directed toward God. He was the reference point, the source of identity, and the center. After the fall, that focus turned inward. Humanity became self-conscious. What had once been a life oriented toward God became a life absorbed with self.

Before the fall, identity was not something to discover or defend —it was received. There was no questioning of worth. No comparison. Life was lived from what God had given.

Afterward, that certainty was lost. Identity became something to secure rather than something to rest in.

This is where insecurity begins.

Self-awareness is more than awareness of self. It is awareness without the stability of God's presence. The soul begins to evaluate, question, and monitor itself. Over time, that inward focus creates pressure. Thoughts grow heavier. Doubt becomes familiar. The need to measure and manage increases.

The mind was never designed to carry that role.

As the self becomes the center, peace begins to fade.

That instability does not remain internal. It begins to shape how others are seen. When identity is uncertain, relationships become strained. People are filtered through comparison, insecurity, and self-protection.

Connection gives way to competition. Openness gives way to caution. Trust becomes difficult to sustain.

What was designed to be natural now requires restoration.

Another shift follows. Before the fall, life flowed from identity. Afterward, life began moving toward identity. Effort replaces rest. Instead of living from what has been given, people begin striving to obtain it—seeking acceptance, value, and security through performance.

The more striving increases, the more distant rest becomes.

This inward focus also affects how we relate to God. Instead of looking toward Him, attention turns back on self. Worth is questioned. Failures are magnified. Drawing near begins to feel uncertain.

Worship becomes self-aware rather than God-centered.

When that shift happens, connection weakens—not because God has moved, but because focus has.

This condition cannot be resolved by improving the self. The issue is not confidence. It is focus.

The way back is not found in fixing the self, but in returning attention to God.

As that shift happens, something changes. The weight of self begins to lift. What once felt overwhelming becomes clearer. What once felt unstable begins to steady.

Freedom is not found by forcing attention away from self. It is found by turning attention toward God.

As He becomes the center again, identity stabilizes. Comparison loses its hold. Performance no longer feels necessary.

The soul returns to what it was created for—to live from God, not from itself.

PART II

WHAT SIN DID TO THE HUMAN HEART

6

THE WOUNDED SELF

Section 1: The Framework of Human Knowing

Every human being interprets reality through a framework. We do not simply see—we process, filter, and interpret. If that framework is distorted, everything that follows becomes unstable.

Before the fall, truth was known effortlessly because relationship with God was unbroken. Truth was not searched for; it was received. Clarity was not achieved; it was lived.

After the fall, that framework fractured, and that fracture still shapes how reality is understood.

Human beings were created to know truth through relationship with God. Before culture, reasoning, or experience, there was His presence and His voice. Truth was not first a concept; it was personal.

Jesus later reveals this fully when He says, "I am the truth" (John 14:6). Truth is not something constructed or mastered—it is Someone encountered.

Once that relationship is disrupted, clarity becomes uncertain.

In the beginning, knowledge flowed from God to humanity. Adam did not discover truth independently; he received it. Revelation came first, and understanding followed.

After the fall, that order reversed. Humanity began relying on reason, experience, and perception apart from God. These can process information, but they cannot fully interpret what is true on their own.

Revelation does not replace thinking—it restores it to its proper place.

Originally, knowledge flowed from intimacy. Learning came through closeness with God, not effort. There was no striving for understanding, only a posture of receiving.

When connection was disrupted, knowledge became something pursued independently, introducing confusion.

Truth was never designed to function apart from its source.

Human beings were not created to generate truth—they were created to receive it.

Truth does not originate from emotion, desire, or opinion—it flows from God. The heart was designed to recognize and respond to His voice, but after the fall, it began trying to produce what it was meant to receive.

At that point, stability is lost.

Before the fall, there was order: the spirit received, the soul interpreted, the body responded.

After the fall, that order reversed. What is external began to lead. Senses, emotions, and thoughts moved forward—and without God, they lack stability.

This is where confusion begins.

Emotions fluctuate. Perception becomes unreliable. Truth feels fragmented.

The issue is not information. It is alignment.

Yet something within still recognizes that this is not how life was meant to function. There is a quiet longing for clarity, for meaning, for something that holds.

That longing is not accidental; it is the echo of original design.

Salvation does more than forgive—it restores. It realigns the human person with God's design.

When relationship is restored, understanding stabilizes, perception begins to heal, and clarity returns.

The goal is not to accumulate knowledge. It is to return to the One from whom truth flows.

Truth becomes clear again when relationship is restored.

Section 2: Reason, Emotion, and Revelation

After the fall, humanity began relying on reason and emotion to interpret reality. Neither was designed to lead. The mind was never meant to be the master, and emotion was never meant to define truth. Only what God reveals does that.

Reason is a gift from God. It allows us to think, analyze, and make sense of what we experience, but it operates within limits. It can only process what is observable and familiar. It cannot move beyond what has been revealed.

This is why Scripture says, "The natural man does not receive the things of the Spirit of God..." (1 Corinthians 2:14). Reason can interpret what God reveals, but it cannot replace revelation.

If placed in that role, something weakens. Faith becomes uncertain, and truth begins to feel unstable.

Emotion is also part of God's design. It allows us to feel, respond, and connect. But after the fall, it became unstable. It reacts to circumstances, memories, and perception—not always to what is true.

Feelings can be real, but they are not always reliable.

When emotion leads, problems appear larger than they are. Situations are misread. Even God's character can be questioned.

Emotion reflects the condition of the soul, but it does not define reality.

Reason and emotion together can help interpret what is happening, but they cannot establish what is true. They shape perception, but perception is not truth.

Without God, interpretation becomes unstable. This is why human understanding shifts so easily—it lacks a fixed source.

Revelation changes that.

Revelation is God speaking truth to the human spirit. It brings clarity where things feel hidden, corrects what has become distorted, and steadies what feels uncertain.

Jesus said, "The Spirit of truth will guide you into all truth" (John 16:13). Revelation restores what was disrupted in the fall. It realigns perception with what is true—not merely what appears.

God's design was always ordered: revelation leads, reason follows, emotion responds.

When that order is restored, something settles. The mind becomes clearer, the heart steadier, and perception regains reliability.

Truth no longer shifts with circumstance. It remains anchored in God.

Spiritual maturity is not the accumulation of knowledge. It is learning to live from revelation—hearing God's voice, trusting His character, and allowing His truth to shape interpretation.

The fall trained humanity to react. The Spirit teaches us to respond.

That difference changes everything.

Section 3: Truth as Relationship, Not Just Information

If reason explains how we think and emotion explains how we feel, revelation points to something deeper. It shows how we truly know. Revelation is not simply information—it is relational.

Truth is not something to master; it is encountered through God.

From the beginning, truth was never meant to exist apart from relationship. Humanity was created to know truth by knowing Him. Truth does not originate in human reasoning, experience, or opinion —it begins with God Himself.

Scripture makes this clear: "God is light" (1 John 1:5). "I am the truth" (John 14:6). Truth is not abstract. It is rooted in God's nature. To know truth, we must know Him.

In Eden, truth was not studied—it was lived. Adam and Eve walked with God, and in that relationship, clarity was natural. There was no need to analyze or search for meaning. Truth was experienced.

This pattern continues throughout Scripture. People walked with God, and as they walked, truth became clear.

Study can support understanding, but it cannot replace relationship.

Truth unfolds in the walk.

God did not send truth as a concept—He revealed it through a person. Jesus embodies truth. His life reveals God's character. His words reveal God's wisdom. His work reveals God's purpose.

Remove Christ, and truth loses stability, because it is not complete apart from Him.

Truth is not discovered through effort alone—it is revealed.

Jesus said, "The Spirit of truth will guide you into all truth" (John 16:13). The Holy Spirit restores what was disrupted in the fall. He brings clarity where there has been distortion, exposes what is false, and aligns us with what is real.

But this requires relationship, listening, and dependence.

Truth is not accessed through control—it is received through connection.

It does not begin in the intellect. It begins in the heart.

Scripture says, "With the heart one believes..." (Romans 10:10). The condition of the heart shapes how truth is received. When the heart is closed or wounded, truth can feel distant or even threatening. When it is open and humble, clarity returns.

The mind then processes what the heart has already received.

The fall distorted perception. Fear, shame, and pride began shaping how reality is seen. Because of this, people struggle with truth—not always because they reject it, but because they cannot see it clearly.

The lens has been damaged.

Relationship with God restores that lens. As perception is healed, truth becomes recognizable again.

Jesus said, "You will know the truth, and the truth will make you free" (John 8:32). Truth is not given simply to inform—it is given to free. It breaks the hold of lies, restores identity, and brings clarity where there has been confusion.

It does not only fill the mind; it transforms life.

When truth is separated from relationship, something essential is lost. It becomes rigid and lifeless, producing knowledge without transformation. This is what Jesus confronted—people who knew Scripture but did not know God.

But when truth remains rooted in relationship, something different forms. Clarity deepens. Transformation follows. The heart begins to change.

Truth is safest when it flows from the One who gives it.

7

THE DISTRACTED SOUL

Section 1: The Limitations of Sight, Sound, Touch, Taste, and Smell

Humanity was given five extraordinary senses—sight, sound, touch, taste, and smell. They anchor us to the physical world. They help us navigate, respond, and experience life. They are a gift from God.

Following the fall, however, these same human senses became unreliable when used as the foundation of truth. They can report what is natural, but they cannot reveal what is spiritual. They show what is happening around us, yet cannot uncover what God is doing beyond it.

The issue is not the senses themselves, but what happens when they begin to lead.

Sight feels authoritative. What is visible often appears final. But Scripture reminds us, "We walk by faith, not by sight" (2 Corinthians 5:7). Sight shows circumstances, obstacles, and limitations, but it cannot reveal what God is doing behind them.

It sees the storm, but not the One who commands it.

When sight becomes primary, fear often follows—because attention fixes on what appears rather than what is true.

Hearing presents a similar challenge. We are surrounded by voices—external and internal. Hearing detects sound, but it does not determine its source. Without discernment, everything begins to carry equal weight—culture, influence, internal thoughts, and surrounding voices all sounding convincing.

This is why Jesus said, "He who has ears to hear, let him hear." Not all hearing leads to understanding. Truth requires more than sound—it requires revelation.

Touch brings a sense of confirmation. What is felt appears real. But faith cannot be built on physical sensation alone.

When faith depends on feeling, it becomes unstable.

God often works in ways that cannot be physically sensed. When feeling becomes the measure of reality, trust weakens.

Desire also plays a role. What draws the heart begins to shape what is pursued. After the fall, desire became misaligned. What does not satisfy is often craved, and what brings life is often resisted.

This is not a failure of truth—it is a misalignment of appetite.

When desire leads, it quietly pulls the soul away from what is good.

The senses are deeply connected to memory, emotion, and experience. They shape responses to life, but they remain limited. They cannot interpret spiritual reality on their own. They cannot discern God's presence or His purposes apart from Him.

They report information, but they do not define truth.

This is the difference between facts and truth. The senses give facts—they report what is happening. Truth comes from God. Truth interprets what the senses report.

Faith does not deny what is seen. It refuses to be ruled by it.

Truth is not established by perception. It is established by God.

From the beginning, there was order: the spirit leads, the soul interprets, the body responds.

After the fall, that order reversed.

When the senses lead, confusion increases. When the Spirit leads, clarity returns.

The senses are not the problem, but they were never meant to lead.

Jesus lived this reality consistently. He did not respond to what appeared—He responded to what was true. He taught His disciples to do the same: not to deny what they saw, but to interpret it through God's presence and promises.

That remains the invitation—not to reject the senses, but to refuse to let them lead.

Section 2: How the Senses Distort Reality After the Fall

After the fall, the senses did not stop functioning, but they stopped interpreting reality correctly. They continued to report what was happening, yet the meaning of what was seen, heard, and felt became distorted.

What was designed to engage with creation became a filter through which reality is misread.

For this reason, people can experience the same situation and arrive at completely different conclusions. The issue is not what is perceived—it is how it is interpreted.

Sight no longer sees clearly. It becomes selective, focusing on what feels threatening, uncertain, or negative. It notices the obstacle but misses what God may be doing beyond it.

This is why fear often begins with what is seen.

The problem is not blindness—it is misinterpretation.

Hearing also became complicated. Humanity is surrounded by many voices—external and internal. Thoughts, past experiences, and outside influences blend together.

Hearing detects sound, but it cannot determine what is true.

Without discernment, everything begins to carry weight. Over time, these voices shape belief.

Hearing truth, therefore, is not automatic—it is learned in relationship with God.

Feeling creates a sense of certainty. What is felt often appears real. But when feeling becomes the measure of reality, faith becomes unstable.

God's presence begins to be interpreted through emotion. If

nothing is felt, He is assumed distant. If emotions overwhelm, something is assumed wrong.

God is not limited to feeling. Truth remains steady, even when emotion fluctuates.

Desire also shifted. What the soul is drawn to is no longer consistently aligned with what it needs. After the fall, desire became misdirected—pulling toward distraction, the temporary, or what reinforces self rather than truth.

When desire is not shaped by truth, it begins to shape life in the wrong direction.

Memory adds another layer. The senses are tied to past experience. Previous moments influence present perception. People respond not only to what is happening now, but to what has already happened.

This is why reactions can feel stronger than the moment itself.

Perception becomes layered.

These distortions do not exist in isolation. They are shaped by experience, fear, past wounds, and what has been reinforced over time.

Because of this, perception becomes filtered. Two people can encounter the same reality and interpret it differently—not because reality has changed, but because their interpretive lens is different.

The enemy does not need to change truth. He only needs to distort perception.

If attention is influenced—what is focused on, what is heard, what is felt—belief begins to shift. Confusion increases. Fear intensifies. Misinterpretation follows.

People begin to misread themselves, others, and even God.

But this is not the end.

Jesus came not only to forgive, but to restore. Throughout His ministry, He restored sight, hearing, and clarity. These were not only physical acts—they revealed something deeper.

God restores the ability to see clearly again.

When perception is restored, truth becomes recognizable.

Section 3: Living by Faith, Not by Senses

As the limitations of the senses are understood, the path forward becomes clear. The Christian life is not led by what is perceived. It is led by faith.

Scripture repeats this consistently: "The just shall live by faith." Not by what is seen, not by what is felt, not by what appears.

The senses report what is natural. Faith connects to what God is doing beyond it.

The senses are tied to what is temporary. They interpret circumstances as they exist in the moment.

Faith reaches beyond that.

Paul writes, "What is seen is temporary, but what is unseen is eternal" (2 Corinthians 4:18). Faith does not ignore what is seen. It places it within the context of what is unseen, anchoring the soul in what does not change.

The senses interpret based on surroundings. Faith interprets based on what God has said.

This is why Abraham could trust God even when everything around him suggested otherwise. He did not deny what he saw—he refused to let it define what was true.

Faith allows life to be lived from God's Word rather than from what is immediately visible.

The senses keep perception at ground level. Faith lifts it.

When Elisha prayed for his servant, nothing in the situation changed—yet everything about how it was seen did. What once produced fear became a place of confidence.

Faith does not always change circumstances immediately, but it changes how they are understood.

The senses fluctuate. They respond to pressure, emotion, and environment.

Faith does not.

It remains steady because it is rooted in God.

This is why Jesus remained at peace in the storm. His perception was not governed by what He saw, but by what He knew.

Faith brings stability where the senses create instability.

It does not silence the senses—it restores order.

The senses can inform, but they cannot lead.

When faith leads, something shifts. Perception becomes clearer. Emotion settles. Decisions align.

The issue is not whether we sense things. It is who is in control.

There are seasons when the senses feel uncertain—moments where nothing seems to change, clarity feels distant, and the visible offers no reassurance.

This is not absence; it is formation.

Faith grows when it is not supported by immediate evidence. Trust deepens when it is no longer dependent on what can be seen or felt.

A life led by the senses is unstable. A life led by faith is anchored.

Faith produces what the senses cannot sustain—clarity in confusion, peace in pressure, trust in uncertainty—because it is rooted in God, not in circumstance.

The Holy Spirit teaches this way of living. He shifts perception from the natural to the spiritual. He leads beyond reaction into response. He restores the ability to interpret life through God's truth.

This is not natural. It is learned.

And it is the life Jesus invites us into.

8

THE DIVIDED HEART

S ection 1: The Inner Compass God Placed Within Us

An awareness exists within every person that does not come from thought, emotion, or the physical senses. Even in those who have never opened Scripture, it quietly makes itself known. It appears as a sense of right and wrong, a pull toward meaning, or an uneasiness when something is not aligned.

It is not loud, but it is persistent.

That awareness is not imagined. It is part of our design. Scripture describes it in different ways—the heart, the conscience, the spirit—but each points to the same reality: human beings were formed with the capacity to perceive beyond what is seen.

Something within responds to truth even before it can be explained.

At the core of a person is not the body, but the spirit. The body engages the visible world. The mind processes experience. The deepest awareness comes from within.

"The spirit of man is the lamp of the LORD" (Proverbs 20:27).

A place exists where God's light meets human awareness. This is why—even apart from Scripture—there is recognition that some things are right and others are not. There is a response to injustice, a sense of what is out of place, and a longing for something beyond what is visible.

That awareness can be ignored or reshaped, but it does not disappear. It reflects that humanity was not created to live only by what is seen.

Discernment begins in this quiet place. It rarely arrives as something dramatic. More often, it appears as a subtle restraint, a lack of peace, or a clarity that does not come from reasoning alone.

Scripture describes this as the Spirit bearing witness within (Romans 8:16).

This is not the mind processing information or emotion reacting to circumstances. It is God communicating within the human spirit.

At times, the senses offer no clarity, yet something within still recognizes direction. Circumstances may be unclear, but inner awareness remains steady. Often this is only recognized in hindsight—realizing something was sensed before it was understood.

That recognition is not emotional. It is spiritual.

This inner capacity was affected by the fall. What was once clear became inconsistent, but not removed.

Through Christ, it is restored.

Salvation does more than forgive—it realigns. The spirit is made alive. The mind begins to renew. The ability to recognize truth strengthens.

Discernment is not the accumulation of information. It is the ability to recognize what is true beneath what appears.

Information can be gathered. Discernment is received.

It allows perception beyond the visible—the direction of a path, the weight of a decision, the presence shaping a moment.

This is how God leads.

His guidance is not limited to external instruction. It unfolds within the person learning to recognize Him.

This inner awareness becomes a quiet guide, bringing clarity, restraint, and direction over time. When ignored, confusion increases. When followed, alignment grows.

God has not left His people without direction. He has placed within them the capacity to recognize His leading. This is not reserved for a few. It is part of what it means to belong to Him.

As a person walks with God, this awareness becomes clearer and steadier—not because it originates within, but because it is anchored in Him.

Section 2: Discernment vs. Instinct

There is a difference between what feels internal and what is truly spiritual. Instinct and discernment can appear similar. Both arise from within and feel immediate and convincing. But they do not come from the same source, and they do not lead in the same direction.

Learning to recognize that difference is essential.

Instinct belongs to the natural condition. It is shaped by experience, memory, and the body's need to protect itself. It reacts to what feels threatening or uncertain—moving away from discomfort and toward what appears safe.

It is not wrong, but it is limited. It can only respond to what has been known and what is perceived in the moment.

Discernment does not function that way. It does not originate in the past or in the body's response to pressure. It comes from the Spirit of God working within a person learning to recognize His voice.

Where instinct reacts, discernment reveals.

It does not move because something feels urgent, but because something is understood—even if quietly.

This is why the two can lead in different directions.

Instinct avoids what feels unfamiliar or uncomfortable. Discernment is not guided by comfort. At times, it leads toward what would naturally be avoided—not recklessly, but with clarity that does not depend on ease.

The difference becomes clearer in what shapes each one. Instinct is formed by what has already happened. Past experiences—especially painful ones—shape how situations are interpreted. A person can respond to the present through the lens of the past without realizing it.

Discernment is not bound to that pattern. It is shaped by what God is revealing now—recognizing what is true in the present moment.

Instinct centers on self-preservation. It asks: What feels safe?

Discernment shifts that focus. It asks: What is true according to God?

Another distinction appears in how each one moves. Instinct often creates urgency, especially when fear is involved.

Discernment does not operate under that pressure. Even when action is required, it carries steadiness not driven by panic. There is clarity without force.

Instinct is easily influenced by external conditions. Stress and surrounding voices shape how it responds.

Discernment, when rooted in the Spirit, remains steady even when circumstances are unsettled.

This is where the deeper difference emerges: instinct can feel right and still lead in the wrong direction. Discernment can feel unfamiliar and still lead in the right one.

If decisions are made based only on what feels natural, it becomes easy to mistake comfort for truth.

Discernment is not developed through effort alone. It grows out of relationship.

Jesus said, "My sheep hear My voice."

As that relationship deepens, the difference becomes clearer. What once felt similar begins to separate. What once seemed uncertain becomes steady.

Section 3: How the Holy Spirit Restores Perception

The fall did more than introduce sin—it distorted how humanity sees. What was once clear became uncertain. What was steady became difficult to recognize.

Jesus came not only to save, but to restore what had been affected. That restoration includes perception, and it unfolds through the work of the Holy Spirit.

When a person is born again, the change reaches deeper than

behavior. The spirit awakens. What was once unresponsive begins to recognize again.

Scripture describes this as the eyes of the heart being opened: "The eyes of your heart may be enlightened" (Ephesians 1:18).

This is where restored perception begins—not with effort, but with awakening.

From there, clarity grows through the Word. Scripture is not simply information to be understood. It is light that reveals. It brings into view what was hidden and corrects what has been misaligned.

"The word of God... discerns the thoughts and intentions of the heart" (Hebrews 4:12).

As the Word takes root, it reshapes how a person sees. Truth becomes recognizable, not abstract.

The Spirit also leads through an inner clarity that cannot always be explained outwardly. At times, this comes as peace—a steady sense that something is aligned. At other times, it comes as conviction—a clear awareness that something is not.

Neither is driven by emotion alone. These are ways the Spirit guides, protecting and redirecting as needed.

What cannot be reasoned through becomes discernible within.

This restoration does not remain static. Discernment grows through response. As a person listens and responds to what is revealed, perception becomes more defined.

Scripture describes maturity as having senses trained to discern both good and evil (Hebrews 5:14). With use, what was once faint becomes clear. What was once uncertain becomes steady.

The Holy Spirit also enables perception that does not depend on the senses. He reveals what lies beneath appearances—what is true beyond what is immediately visible.

This includes recognizing direction, identifying what is not aligned, and understanding what God is doing within a moment.

This is not heightened emotion. It is deeper awareness.

As this develops, the focus of discernment shifts. It is no longer centered on identifying what is wrong, but on recognizing what is true. That truth is found in Christ.

The Spirit does not draw attention inward for its own sake. He directs it toward Him. His voice becomes more recognizable. His direction more discernible. His character becomes the measure of all things.

The result is not simply improved awareness, but restored relationship. Clarity replaces confusion. Direction replaces uncertainty.

But even this is not the final goal.

Discernment is not given for independence. It is given for relationship.

What was once obscured becomes clear again—not for control, but for communion.

9

THE FEARFUL MIND

Section 1: How Culture Shapes Our View of Reality

Culture shapes how a person sees long before they realize it. What feels natural is often learned and reinforced over time. Because it is familiar, it is rarely questioned.

Yet familiarity does not make something true.

Every culture carries its own way of interpreting life. It forms assumptions about what matters, what is acceptable, and what should be pursued.

These do not remain external. They become a lens through which reality is understood.

What one person considers normal, another may see differently —not because reality has changed, but because the lens has.

This shaping begins early. Long before conscious decisions are made, patterns are already forming. Ways of responding, understanding authority, and measuring success are absorbed over time.

These patterns settle into the inner life and begin to feel like truth.

By the time they are recognized, they are no longer experienced as influences, but as reality.

Culture also shapes what is valued. Certain pursuits are elevated, while others are overlooked. Success may be defined by achievement or independence. Comfort may become a measure of well-being.

These values are often followed without question—not because they have been examined, but because they have been normalized.

This influence extends into how Scripture is understood. No one approaches it without perspective. Cultural assumptions affect how authority is viewed, how suffering is interpreted, and how God is perceived.

Two people can read the same passage and arrive at different conclusions—not because truth has changed, but because their lens remains unexamined.

The Spirit is necessary.

He reveals what culture cannot.

Repeated ideas begin to feel settled. Beliefs about identity, worth, and purpose can take shape without being consciously chosen. When something is heard often enough, it becomes difficult to distinguish whether it is true or simply familiar.

Truth does not become true through repetition.

It must be revealed.

The strongest influences are often the least visible. Cultural blind spots do not feel like limitations—they feel normal. Because they are shared, they are rarely challenged and can even be reinforced in spiritual environments.

Without discernment, a person may not recognize what is shaping perception.

Jesus did not ignore culture. He confronted what was false and restored what was true. He challenged assumptions and revealed a different way of seeing—while still speaking through what was familiar to point beyond it.

When a person comes to Christ, identity shifts. Culture no longer holds final authority. It does not disappear, but it is no longer the foundation.

A new lens begins to form, shaped by relationship with God.

As that shift takes place, perception changes. What once felt unquestioned is reconsidered. What was hidden begins to come into view.

Section 2: Tradition as a Teacher—and a Thief

Tradition carries influence deeper than it first appears. It shapes how people think, live, and relate to God. Because it is familiar, it is rarely questioned.

What has always been present can begin to feel inherently true.

Yet Scripture makes a clear distinction: tradition is only trustworthy when it aligns with truth.

Every tradition begins with meaning. It may come from a genuine encounter, a faithful practice, or a way of remembering what God has done.

Over time, what was once lived becomes repeated. What is repeated becomes expected. Eventually, it can take on authority—not because God declared it, but because it has always been there.

Here the shift becomes subtle.

What began as a response to truth can start to stand in its place.

Not all tradition is harmful. When it remains rooted in truth, it can preserve what matters, reinforce faith, and carry understanding across generations. It becomes a way of remembering, not replacing.

The difficulty arises when that order changes. When tradition begins to define truth rather than reflect it, something is lost.

Jesus confronted this directly: "You nullify the Word of God for the sake of your tradition" (Matthew 15:6).

What was meant to guide had become restrictive. Instead of leading people toward God, it began to limit their response to Him.

This influence often shapes expectations in ways that are not immediately visible. Many beliefs about God are formed not from Scripture itself, but from what has been passed down. These expectations begin to define what is considered possible, acceptable, or even faithful.

When those expectations are narrow, the ability to recognize what God is doing becomes limited.

Familiarity plays a role here. What feels normal is rarely examined. Over time, this creates resistance—not always intentional, but deeply rooted.

When something challenges what has long been accepted, it can feel wrong simply because it is unfamiliar.

This is what made it difficult for many to recognize Jesus. They were not lacking knowledge—their expectations had already been formed.

Tradition can also shape how a person understands their standing before God. It can produce confidence based on outward patterns, where faith is measured by adherence rather than relationship.

At the same time, it can create burden, where people feel weighed down by expectations never established by God.

In both cases, the focus shifts away from Christ.

Yet Scripture reminds us: "There is now no condemnation..." (Romans 8:1).

What God establishes through grace cannot be replaced by what is maintained through pattern.

Throughout Scripture, God brings alignment where things have shifted. He does not discard everything passed down, but He does not allow it to stand above truth.

When tradition supports truth, it is preserved. When it obscures or replaces it, it is confronted.

The Spirit brings clarity, revealing what should remain and what should be released.

The goal is not the removal of tradition, but its proper place. It can serve when it points beyond itself.

It becomes harmful when it attempts to define what only God can establish.

When submitted to Him, it can guide.

But truth must always remain the authority.

Section 3: Letting Scripture Break Cultural Blindness

Culture and tradition shape perception, often without being recognized. Over time, assumptions settle into place and begin to feel like truth. They are not questioned because they are familiar.

That is what makes them difficult to see.

What is inherited can feel natural, even when it is not aligned. Because of this, transformation requires more than sincerity. It requires exposure to truth.

Scripture does not emerge from culture. It stands above it. When it speaks, it does not affirm what is already assumed—it reveals what is actually true.

Paul describes transformation as the renewing of the mind (Romans 12:2). Renewal begins when what has been accepted is brought into the light of what God has said. Without that, change remains surface-level.

The Word does more than inform. It reveals. It reaches beneath behavior into what shapes it.

"The word of God is living and active... discerning the thoughts and intentions of the heart" (Hebrews 4:12).

It brings into view not only actions, but the beliefs behind them.

This is where cultural influence is uncovered.

Every person lives within a story formed over time. Family, culture, and experience shape identity and interpretation. These patterns begin to feel fixed, as though they define reality.

Yet not every story reflects truth.

Scripture introduces a different foundation—one that does not adjust to what has been inherited, but replaces it with what is true.

This process is not always comfortable. What has long been accepted can be difficult to question. Familiar patterns can feel right simply because they are known.

Yet Scripture brings clarity where comfort has misled. It reveals what has gone unnoticed and brings it into view.

This is why David prayed for God to search his heart. What is hidden must be seen before it can be changed.

As Scripture is allowed to lead, tradition is no longer treated as authority. It is examined in the light of truth. What aligns is strength-ened. What does not is released.

This reflects the same tension Jesus addressed—what has been accepted must respond to truth.

With this, identity begins to shift. It is no longer grounded in culture, history, or expectation, but in Christ.

"If anyone is in Christ, he is a new creation" (2 Corinthians 5:17).

This does more than change behavior. It changes perception. What once defined a person begins to lose its authority.

As the Word takes root, it becomes a point of reference within. It begins to distinguish between influences—what is cultural, what is emotional, and what is spiritual.

Discernment becomes clearer—not through effort alone, but through truth being internalized. What once felt confusing begins to settle into clarity.

This process is guided by the Spirit. Jesus said the Spirit would lead into all truth (John 16:13). He does not merely explain Scripture —He brings it to life within the person.

What could remain information becomes lived and understood.

The result is not simply correction, but clarity. As the lens is restored, perception begins to change. What once felt normal is re-evaluated. What once seemed unclear becomes visible.

The focus shifts away from what has been inherited and toward Christ.

Truth is not only something to understand—it is Someone to know.

10

ENVIRONMENT, SEASONS, AND TRAUMA

Section 1: The Invisible Realm—What Scripture Reveals About the Unseen World

Most people live as if what they see is all that exists. The visible world feels immediate and stable, giving the impression that it is the most reliable measure of reality.

Scripture presents something different.

"What is seen is temporary, but what is unseen is eternal" (2 Corinthians 4:18).

What appears solid is not ultimate—it is the surface, shaped by something deeper.

This shifts how reality is understood.

The unseen is not distant or secondary. It precedes what is visible and gives rise to it.

Scripture makes this clear: "What is seen was not made out of things which are visible" (Hebrews 11:3).

The physical world is not self-originating. It expresses what exists beyond it.

Because of this, the unseen realm is not abstract. It is ordered and active. Scripture describes the presence of God, the activity of angels, and the reality of spiritual forces—not as symbolic ideas, but as part of reality itself.

What cannot be seen is not inactive; it is continually at work.

Human beings were not created unaware of this. In the beginning, there was clarity—an awareness of God and His presence. After the fall, that clarity diminished. Perception narrowed. Attention shifted to what is observable.

Yet that awareness is not gone. It can be restored.

Paul prays, "The eyes of your heart may be enlightened" (Ephesians 1:18).

This is not imagination. It is restored perception.

Within this unseen realm, there is also conflict. Scripture does not describe it as neutral. "We do not wrestle against flesh and blood" (Ephesians 6:12).

What appears purely physical is often connected to something deeper.

This does not remove human responsibility, but it reveals that events are not limited to what is seen.

Jesus did not treat this realm as distant. He engaged with it directly. "He disarmed the rulers and authorities" (Colossians 2:15).

What operates in the unseen is not beyond His authority; it is subject to Him.

What unfolds in the visible world is not isolated. Scripture consistently shows that events, struggles, and outcomes are connected to deeper realities.

The visible reflects what is already in motion.

Believers are called to live with awareness. To walk by faith is not to ignore what is seen, but to understand it in light of what is unseen.

Situations are no longer interpreted only by what can be measured or felt. They are viewed through the recognition that God is at work beyond what can be observed.

Truth does not originate from what is visible. It comes from God—who is unseen, yet the source of all that is real.

If perception remains limited to what is seen, understanding will remain incomplete.

As the unseen is recognized, clarity begins to form.

Reality is not defined by appearance, but by what God reveals.

Section 2: Angels, Demons, and Heavenly Order

Recognizing the unseen realm leads to a deeper question: what exists within it?

Scripture does not describe this realm as empty, but as structured and ordered. It reflects purpose, authority, and assignment. What cannot be seen is not chaotic; it is governed.

Angels are part of this order. They are not symbolic forces, but created beings operating in alignment with God. Scripture presents them as active—carrying out His commands, delivering what He reveals, and serving within His purposes.

"His angels... who do His commandments" (Psalm 103:20).

Their activity is not independent. It reflects the authority under which they operate.

This reveals something about God's kingdom: it is intentional and ordered.

Scripture indicates distinctions in role and responsibility, though not fully explained. There are hints of leadership, worship, service, and protection. The details are not the focus; the pattern is.

God's kingdom is not random. It moves according to design.

Within this design, activity is often specific. Scripture shows moments where angelic involvement is connected to particular people, places, and situations.

This suggests interaction between the unseen and the visible—not always observable, but consistently aligned with God's purposes.

Scripture also speaks of opposition. Demons are not equal to God, nor independent in power. They are fallen beings, operating in distortion of their original design.

Their influence is seen in deception and resistance to truth. Where God brings clarity, they seek to obscure. Where truth is revealed, they attempt to distort.

Their activity, however, is limited.

They do not operate without boundary.

Even in opposition, there is structure—not rooted in truth, but imitating what God established. There is coordination, but it is not grounded in what is real. It is a distortion, not a counterpart.

This distinction matters.

Not everything that appears organized is aligned with truth.

Scripture describes real conflict within this realm—not symbolic, but actual. There are moments where resistance is present and where outcomes are shaped beyond what can be seen.

This does not mean everything is spiritualized, but it does mean not everything can be explained at the surface level.

Clarity comes in understanding where authority rests. "He disarmed the rulers and authorities" (Colossians 2:15).

Christ's authority is complete.

Everything within this realm is subject to Him, whether in alignment or opposition.

Because of this, the believer's position is not uncertain. Authority is not based on feeling or experience. It is based on what has already been established.

Scripture describes believers as seated with Him.

The struggle is not to gain authority, but to live from it.

The unseen may be active, but it is not ultimate.

As this becomes clear, confusion begins to lift. What once felt unclear takes shape. Patterns are recognized. Discernment sharpens.

The visible world is no longer the only reference point.

Section 3: Why the Unseen Realm Still Affects Us Today

The unseen realm is not confined to the past. What Scripture reveals continues. What cannot be seen is not inactive—it must be understood differently.

Scripture describes an ongoing reality. Believers are called to remain alert, stand firm, and resist. These instructions reflect something present, not historical.

The struggle may not always be recognized, but it has not disappeared.

Human beings exist at the intersection of what is seen and unseen. They are not only physical, but spiritual. Because of this, what happens within a person carries weight beyond what is outwardly visible.

Thoughts, responses, and decisions are not isolated. They are part of something deeper.

Scripture warns against giving place to what is destructive. Influence is not automatic; it is either allowed or resisted.

There are moments when something is sensed without being fully understood. Certain environments feel unsettled. Others carry a sense of peace.

These are not always emotional responses.

Scripture shows that God's presence brings order and peace, while what is misaligned produces unrest.

What surrounds a person can affect how they think and respond, even when the source is not clear.

The patterns described in Scripture have not changed. Deception, distortion, and accusation still shape perception. What began in the beginning continues in different forms.

Without awareness, these patterns repeat.

What is familiar is not always understood.

Scripture does not present only opposition. It reveals provision. God is not distant from what unfolds. His activity continues, even when not perceived.

The unseen is not empty. It includes both resistance and help.

The most important shift is not what surrounds the believer, but what is within.

The presence of God changes how a person relates to what is unseen. They are not defined by environment. They are positioned within it differently.

Light does not adjust to darkness.

It reveals it.

Prayer becomes part of this reality. It is not symbolic; it is participatory. Scripture shows that what happens in prayer connects to what unfolds beyond what can be seen.

It aligns the believer with God's activity.

Through that alignment, what is unseen is engaged—not always visibly, but truly.

Because of Christ, the believer is not an observer. Authority is not achieved; it is established.

It is lived from, not worked toward.

This changes how challenges are approached.

What is unseen may be active, but it is not ultimate.

Understanding this does not produce fear.

It produces clarity.

Situations are no longer viewed only at the surface level, but in light of what may be taking place beyond it.

Awareness replaces confusion.

What is unseen is not greater than Christ—but it is real enough that it cannot be ignored.

PART III

A WORLD BROKEN BY KNOWLEDGE

11

THE INVISIBLE REALM

Section 1: How Atmospheres Shape Human Behavior
Most people assume their responses come only from within—thoughts, past experiences, or immediate circumstances. Scripture points to something deeper. Human behavior is not formed in isolation. It is influenced by what surrounds a person, both seen and unseen.

What feels like a personal reaction is often shaped by a larger environment.

Atmosphere is more than mood. It is an environment that affects the inner life. Just as the body responds to physical conditions, the inner person responds to what cannot be measured directly.

This is why certain places feel different without a clear explanation. Some carry tension or heaviness. Others bring clarity or peace.

These differences are not random—they reflect influence.

Scripture suggests these environments are not accidental. They form over time through what is present and what is allowed to remain. The presence of God, patterns of behavior, and the direction of a community all contribute to what develops.

What begins as influence can become a kind of climate—something that feels normal, even when it is not aligned.

Environment shapes how people think and respond. Reactions that seem personal may be influenced by what surrounds them. Moments of pressure, confusion, or unexpected clarity are not always internal.

They can reflect the atmosphere a person has entered.

Without awareness, it becomes easy to assume everything originates from within—when there is more at work.

Jesus did not ignore this. He did not move through environments unchanged. Where there was confusion, He brought clarity. Where there was oppression, He brought freedom. Where there was fear, He brought peace.

His presence did not adjust to what surrounded Him—it altered it.

What was established shifted in response to Him.

Scripture also shows that not every environment responds the same way. Some resist what God is doing. This resistance is not a limitation of His power, but a reflection of what has been established over time.

Patterns of unbelief or disorder can shape how truth is received.

Discernment is essential here.

Without it, a person may not recognize why something feels resistant or unsettled.

These patterns are often inherited. Families, communities, and cultures carry ways of thinking and responding that persist over time. What feels normal is often repeated long enough to go unquestioned.

These environments shape identity and expectation without conscious awareness.

Recognizing this is where change begins.

Atmosphere is not limited to individual spaces. It can extend across entire communities. Different places carry different influences. Some draw people toward clarity. Others reinforce confusion.

This does not remove personal responsibility, but it explains why patterns appear in certain environments.

Spiritual maturity includes awareness of influence. It is not only about recognizing right and wrong, but understanding what is shaping perception and response.

Without awareness, influence remains unrecognized.

The goal is not to absorb every environment, but to carry something different into it.

Scripture describes believers as light. Light does not adapt to darkness—it reveals it.

This is the difference between being shaped by what surrounds you and becoming a presence that changes it.

Section 2: Territorial Spirits and Regions of Influence

The unseen realm does not operate without order. Scripture presents it as structured, with influence that can extend beyond individuals into regions, communities, and recurring patterns.

What is often described in natural terms as culture or behavior can, at times, reflect something deeper beneath the surface.

Scripture points to this in specific moments. In Daniel 10, resistance is described not as human, but as connected to a spiritual authority associated with a region.

The struggle was real, but its source was not visible.

This reveals that influence is not always individual. Broader patterns can shape entire areas.

This helps explain why certain patterns repeat. Some struggles appear consistently within specific places or across generations. While often explained naturally, Scripture suggests something more may be involved.

Influence can become established over time. What is repeated begins to feel normal, and what feels normal is rarely questioned.

Scripture makes clear, however, that influence is not without boundary. It does not act independently or without access.

What is permitted can grow.

Small openings, left unaddressed, can develop into patterns that become difficult to recognize over time.

What begins personally can extend outward if continually reinforced.

Environment plays a role in this. Where a person lives and

engages affects what they encounter. Different places carry different influences.

This does not remove responsibility, but it explains why similar struggles appear in similar environments.

Not everything originates from within.

Some things are encountered.

The same can be seen within families. Patterns persist across time, shaping expectations and responses. Scripture acknowledges this: what continues unchallenged often continues unchanged.

But this is not permanent.

What is confronted can be broken.

Communities reflect this as well. Groups, churches, and regions develop patterns that either align with truth or resist it. This affects how truth is received.

The same message can be heard differently depending on what has been established.

The condition of the environment matters.

Influence is not fixed. What is reinforced grows stronger. What is confronted loses ground. Where disorder is tolerated, it expands. Where truth is established, clarity takes its place.

Alignment with God determines what becomes established.

Clarity comes in recognizing where authority rests. Believers are not victims of influence. They are in Christ.

Authority is not generated through effort—it is lived from through alignment with Him.

Influence is not something to fear, but something to understand and confront.

As this becomes clear, confusion decreases. Patterns are no longer accepted without question. Discernment sharpens.

What is unseen may shape what is happening, but it does not determine the outcome.

It does not have the final word.

Section 3: How Believers Carry God's Presence Into These Realms

The unseen realm is not only something to understand—it is something believers influence.

Wherever a believer goes, they do not arrive alone—not because of personal strength, but because of who dwells within them. What they carry is not their own. It is the presence of God.

Scripture makes this clear: "The Kingdom of God is within you" (Luke 17:21). "You are God's temple..." (1 Corinthians 3:16).

God's presence is no longer confined to a place. It is carried by His people.

The believer does not enter environments empty.

Something greater is already present before anything is said or done.

Influence often begins before action. There are moments when environments shift in ways that cannot be easily explained. Peace settles where there was tension. Clarity emerges where there was confusion.

This is not personality.

It is presence.

Light does not announce itself.

It reveals what surrounds it.

This presence is not passive. It is connected to what has been established in Christ.

Jesus said, "I give you authority..." (Luke 10:19).

That authority is not based on feeling, but on position. Scripture describes believers as seated with Christ. They do not approach situations from uncertainty, but from what has already been secured.

In this way, the believer becomes a point of connection between what is unseen and what is visible. Through their life, what God desires begins to take shape within real environments.

This is not limited to outward action. It is expressed through how they live, how they respond, and how they remain aligned with truth.

Their presence creates space where change can begin.

This also changes how environments are understood. They no longer define the believer.

They become something the believer engages differently.

Influence does not always appear dramatic.

Often, it begins quietly.

What is carried within begins to affect what is around—peace replacing tension, clarity replacing confusion.

What determines the depth of that influence is not effort, but alignment.

As a believer walks with God, what is within begins to flow outward. This is not forced. It is the result of relationship. Through obedience, prayer, and trust, what God has placed within them becomes evident in what surrounds them.

Understanding this changes how a person moves through the world. They no longer react to every environment as though it defines them.

They become aware of what they carry into it.

This produces steadiness instead of fear, clarity instead of confusion.

The unseen may be active, but it is not greater than what God has placed within His people.

What surrounds them is real, but it is not ultimate.

The presence they carry is.

12

THE HEAVENS

Section 1: The First, Second, and Third Heavens—A Biblical Map
Heaven is often understood as a single place—distant and undefined.

Scripture presents something more structured. It points to distinct dimensions—connected, yet different in function—revealing how reality is ordered.

When Paul speaks of being "caught up to the third heaven" (2 Corinthians 12:2), he is not describing a vague experience. He indicates that what is called heaven is not singular in expression.

There is structure.

The first heaven is what is visible. It includes the sky, the atmosphere, and the natural world as experienced through the senses. Genesis refers to this expanse as heaven, reflecting the creative work of God.

It is measurable and accessible, yet not the source of reality.

What is seen does not originate within itself.

It is the expression of something deeper.

Beyond this is a realm that cannot be seen, yet is consistently described in Scripture as active. This is where spiritual influence operates. It is the place of resistance, deception, and conflict.

Daniel's account points to this—showing that what unfolds there can affect what is experienced in the visible world.

It is also the realm Paul refers to when he speaks of a struggle not against flesh and blood.

Though unseen, it is not inactive.

Above both is the third heaven—the place of God's presence. This is not a realm of conflict, but of completeness. Here, truth is not contested and authority is not challenged.

What originates here is not subject to distortion.

When Paul describes being taken into this dimension, he is pointing to a reality where things are seen as they truly are—without interference.

These dimensions are not disconnected.

They are layered.

The visible is influenced by what is unseen, and what is unseen ultimately answers to what is established in God.

This reveals a consistent pattern:

What is physical reflects what is spiritual.

What is contested is not final.

What is established in God remains unchanged.

Understanding this brings clarity.

What appears purely natural is no longer viewed in isolation. Delays, resistance, and even breakthrough are seen within a larger context.

This does not complicate life.

It defines it.

Scripture also speaks of position. Believers are described as being with Christ. Identity is not anchored in what is seen, but in what is established beyond it.

The visible may shift. The unseen may be active.

But what is rooted in God does not move.

Jesus stands at the center of this reality. He entered the visible world, overcame what operated within the unseen, and returned to the place of authority.

Through Him, what was separated is brought back into alignment.

Access is restored—not only in relationship, but in understanding.

These distinctions are not given to create complexity, but to reveal order. They show that what is seen is not all there is, and that what is established in God is not uncertain.

Restoration is not only about forgiveness—it is about clarity.

As perception is restored, alignment follows.

Section 2: Why God Created a Multi-Layered Universe

Scripture does not present the heavens as abstract. They are intentional.

The structure revealed is ordered and purposeful—not incidental.

This layered design is not simply a detail of creation. It reflects something about God Himself.

Creation reflects its source.

The depth and structure of the heavens point to a God who is not limited or contained. What is seen is not flat because its origin is not simple. Order within creation speaks of precision—and of a nature beyond full comprehension.

The layers do not complicate reality.

They reveal its depth.

From the beginning, God creates through distinction. Light is separated from darkness. Heaven is distinguished from earth. In the same way, the different heavens are not divisions of distance, but distinctions of purpose.

The visible realm is where human life unfolds. The unseen is where influence operates. The highest is where God's presence is fully revealed.

This structure is not arbitrary.

It is aligned with function.

Each layer reveals something different about God.

The visible reflects His creativity and power.

The unseen reveals His authority and governance.

The highest reveals His holiness and completeness.

Together, they form a fuller expression of who He is.

No single layer carries the whole picture, but each contributes to it.

This design also reflects precision. Different forms of life exist within different realms, each suited to its environment. What is physical belongs within what is visible. What is spiritual operates within what is unseen.

The highest realm is not shared in the same way, because it is where God's presence is fully expressed.

Each layer is fitted to what it carries.

The structure also serves a purpose often overlooked:

It allows God to be known without overwhelming what He has created.

Scripture shows that even limited encounters with His presence can exceed what the human frame can endure. What appears as distance is often mercy.

The layered design allows relationship to exist without destruction—revealing truth progressively.

Scripture consistently presents heaven as a kingdom. Where there is a kingdom, there is order—authority, alignment, and purpose.

This pattern is not confined to what is unseen. It is reflected in what unfolds within the visible world.

What God establishes beyond sight becomes the model for what takes shape within it.

The fall introduced separation within this order. What had been aligned became divided.

The work of Christ restores what was broken. He bridges what had been separated, bringing connection between what is seen and what is unseen.

Scripture describes believers as being with Him. Identity is not confined to one realm. They live within the visible—but are anchored beyond it.

This structure is not given only to describe reality.

It reshapes perspective.

Scripture calls the believer to look beyond what is immediate—not to escape the world, but to understand it clearly.

The visible is not the full picture.

It is part of something greater.

The layered heavens reveal intention. They show that creation is ordered, that God is purposeful, and that what is seen is not all there is.

As this becomes understood, perception shifts. What once seemed complete is recognized as partial. What once seemed distant becomes central.

Reality is no longer defined by what is seen alone—but by what God has established beyond it.

Section 3: What These Realms Reveal About God's Plan

The structure of the heavens is not given simply to describe reality. It reveals something about God Himself.

It shows how He governs, orders what He has made, and relates to it.

At the center is relationship.

The layered design does not suggest distance for its own sake, but a way for God to engage with what He has created. He is above all, yet not removed.

From the beginning, this was evident. God walked with humanity. His presence was not hidden behind complexity, but expressed within creation.

What exists was not formed for separation, but for connection.

The fall altered that pattern. What had been aligned became strained. The visible world reflected disorder. The unseen became a place of resistance.

Yet what is established in God did not change.

This contrast reveals the nature of redemption. It is not only about individuals, but about restoring what has been disrupted.

Scripture speaks of reconciliation in a way that extends beyond the personal—pointing to a restoration that brings what has been divided back into alignment.

Life cannot be understood only by what is seen. There is movement beyond the surface—and purpose beyond what is immediately recognized.

This does not complicate reality.

It deepens it.

It places human experience within a larger context, where actions and decisions connect to something greater than the moment itself.

The heavens also reveal that creation is not governed by chance. There is order. What unfolds is not random, but shaped by authority and intention.

Scripture consistently presents reality as a kingdom—structured, directed, and purposeful.

What is established at the highest level shapes what takes place below.

Within this order, humanity has a place.

People are not isolated within creation. They are connected to it. They were created to live in relationship with God and to reflect His order within the world.

Though that calling was disrupted, it was not removed.

Through Christ, it is restored.

This means human life carries purpose that extends beyond what is visible.

This structure also points forward. It reveals the direction in which everything is moving.

Scripture describes a future not defined by separation, but by restoration.

What is fractured will be made whole.

What is divided will be brought together.

The presence of God, once partially known, will be fully realized.

As this becomes understood, perspective shifts.

Life is no longer seen as isolated events, but as part of a connected story. What seems random takes on meaning. What seems uncertain is placed within a larger movement—one that begins with God and ultimately returns to Him.

The heavens do not complicate truth.

They clarify it.

They reveal a God who is ordered, intentional, and relational. They show that creation is structured with purpose and that what is seen is not all there is.

The goal has never been distance—but restoration.

And everything moves toward that end.

13

GOD AND THE MYSTERY OF TIME

Section I: The Nature of Time—God Outside the Clock

Time feels natural because it is how life is experienced. Everything is measured through it—days, seasons, and years. It gives structure to what is done and meaning to what passes.

Scripture presents something different.

Time is not ultimate.

It is created.

God is not bound by it. He stands outside what unfolds moment by moment.

The opening words of Scripture establish this:

"In the beginning, God created..." (Genesis 1:1).

Time begins within that statement.

God does not.

What has a beginning is not eternal, and what is created is not the source.

Time exists because God brought it into being. What is experienced in sequence, He sees in completeness.

This creates a difference in how time is known.

Human life unfolds within limits. Time is experienced through change—growth, delay, and passing moments that cannot be retrieved. Everything is shaped by movement from one point to another.

God does not experience time this way.

He is not moving through it.

He governs it.

Scripture says:

"With the Lord one day is as a thousand years..." (2 Peter 3:8).

This is not a different measurement, but a different relationship.

What unfolds over time for us is not unfolding for Him in the same way.

Yet God is not distant from what He created. He enters time—not because He is limited by it, but because He chooses to engage within it. He meets people within moments, seasons, and history.

This is how He makes Himself known.

The clearest expression is Christ.

The eternal entered what is temporary so that what is temporary could be restored.

God's involvement in time is not constraint.

It is relationship.

God's timing often feels difficult to understand. What appears as delay from our perspective is not absence. What feels like silence is not inactivity.

We see the moment as it is.

God sees where it leads.

The difference is not in what is happening, but in how it is perceived.

Where we see interruption, He sees preparation. Where we see uncertainty, He sees completion.

Waiting becomes part of the process.

Scripture does not present growth as rushed. What God forms takes shape over time—not because He is slow, but because formation cannot be forced.

Lives are developed, not assembled. Character is established, not imposed.

What appears delayed is often the space where something necessary is being formed.

Time can also feel like loss. Moments pass, and what seems possible in one season may no longer appear within reach.

Scripture presents a different understanding.

God is not confined by what has already occurred. What appears beyond recovery to us is not beyond His reach. He restores what seems lost—not by reversing time, but by redeeming what it has carried.

Time is not meaningless. Though temporary, it is part of something larger. What is done within it carries weight beyond it.

Scripture calls us to live with that awareness—to look beyond what is immediate and recognize that each moment connects to something that continues.

Peace begins when time is no longer the reference point. When trust shifts from what can be measured to the One who holds it, perspective changes.

What once felt delayed loses its weight. What once felt uncertain begins to settle.

God is not responding to time as we experience it.

He is directing it according to what He has already established.

Section 2: Why We Struggle With God's Timing

One of the deepest tensions in the Christian life is the difference between our sense of time and God's.

This tension appears throughout Scripture and continues in every generation. It does not come from inconsistency in God, but from limitation in how we perceive what He is doing.

Human life is experienced moment by moment. Progress, loss, and expectation are measured through what unfolds in sequence.

What has not happened yet feels delayed. What has passed feels fixed.

Everything is interpreted within time.

God does not relate to time this way.

He governs it.

What feels late to us is not late to Him—because He is not confined to the same frame of reference.

This difference is not only understood.

It is felt.

After the fall, the human response to time was affected. Waiting became difficult. Trust became unstable. The impulse shifted toward control, urgency, and self-direction.

Impatience is not simply habit.

It reflects a deeper tension between what is experienced and what is trusted.

The world reinforces this tension. Speed is expected. Delay is treated as failure. Results are measured by how quickly they appear.

Waiting is rarely seen as meaningful.

Scripture presents a different pattern.

What God develops is not rushed. Growth unfolds. Formation takes shape over time.

What appears slow is often intentional.

When time stretches, something within becomes visible.

Expectations surface. Motives become clear. Fears that were hidden begin to appear.

This is not incidental.

It is part of the process.

Waiting does not create these things—it reveals them.

What is revealed can then be addressed.

God's timing often feels difficult to understand. It does not always align with what seems logical or efficient.

There are moments that appear too late, too uncertain, or unresolved. Yet these are often the moments where something deeper is taking place.

God is not responding to what is visible alone.

He is working within a larger purpose not limited to the moment.

We often think of timing in terms of outcome—the answer, the breakthrough, the next step.

Scripture shows that timing also involves formation.

What is happening within a person during the process matters.

Time is not only moving life forward.

It is shaping who a person is becoming.

The process carries weight—not just the result.

At its core, the struggle with timing is a struggle with trust.

When trust is unsettled, time feels heavy and uncertain. When trust becomes steady, the pressure of time begins to lessen.

Scripture consistently connects waiting with trust—not because waiting is easy, but because trust anchors what cannot yet be seen.

As this takes hold, perspective shifts.

Waiting is no longer interpreted as absence.

It becomes part of how God works.

What once felt wasted is recognized as purposeful.

Delay is not empty.

It is being used.

Section 3: How God's Timing Shapes Our Faith

Waiting is not empty. It is often the place where much of God's work takes shape.

What appears as delay is not absence—it is space.

Space where faith is formed, refined, and strengthened.

God is not only preparing outcomes.

He is preparing the people who will receive them.

Seasons of waiting bring clarity to what is already within. What is trusted, what is expected, and where hesitation remains begin to surface.

Questions that remain quiet in certainty become visible in uncertainty:

Do we trust God's wisdom when we do not understand?

Do we trust His character when the outcome is not yet seen?

These questions are not raised for condemnation, but for growth.

What is revealed can be strengthened.

Much of this formation happens beneath the surface. It is not always visible and does not always feel like progress.

Yet it is not inactive.

Character, endurance, humility, and dependence are not formed quickly.

They take shape over time.

What feels slow is often intentional.

God forms what is carried before He releases what is being asked for.

There are also dimensions of timing that extend beyond the individual.

God is not working within a single life in isolation. He is aligning people, circumstances, and moments in ways that cannot always be seen at once.

What appears delayed may involve preparation beyond what is visible.

Timing is not only personal.

It is connected.

At times, what is experienced as delay is also protection.

There are moments when what is desired is not yet right, or not yet safe.

God sees what cannot be seen.

What feels withheld is not always denied.

It is often being held until it can be received rightly.

As waiting continues, the tension between control and trust becomes clearer.

There is a choice—to press forward through effort or to rest within what God is doing.

Surrender is not passivity.

It is alignment.

It is where striving gives way to trust.

When that shift takes place, something changes internally.

Pressure begins to lift. Peace begins to settle.

When what has been promised comes into view, it is not only the outcome that has changed.

The person receiving it has been shaped in the process.

Perspective is different. Gratitude is deeper. Trust has been strengthened.

The process affects how the promise is carried.

Over time, focus begins to shift. Attention moves away from

measuring how long something is taking and toward knowing God more fully.

Waiting becomes less about when something will happen and more about what is taking place within.

Strength is not found in control—but in relationship.

God's timing is not delay.

It is design.

It is not withholding—it is preparation.

What unfolds is not random.

It is intentional.

The goal is not only that something happens—but that we are ready when it does.

14

HUMAN WEAKNESS
AND DIVINE STRENGTH

Section 1: The Antediluvian World

When readers encounter the long lifespans in Genesis, the first response is often uncertainty. Living for hundreds of years can seem exaggerated or symbolic.

Yet Scripture presents these ages plainly—without qualification or explanation.

The question is not simply whether they lived that long, but why such longevity was possible.

The world from Adam to Noah was not the same as the one now known. It existed closer to the original design of creation. Humanity, though affected by the fall, had not yet experienced the full weight of its consequences.

Adam lived 930 years, and others followed with similarly extended lives. This suggests that what God created was still operating with strength not yet fully diminished.

Human life was not designed to be fragile.

The body was created without disease, decay, or internal breakdown.

After the fall, death entered—but it did not take hold immediately in its full expression. Aging began, yet unfolded slowly. What had been created with strength continued to sustain life, even as deterioration had begun.

That strength weakened gradually.

The environment also played a role. The early world appears to have functioned under conditions that supported life in ways no longer present.

Scripture points to a stability within creation different from what is now experienced.

The earth was not subject to the same extremes or pressures that now contribute to decline. What surrounded humanity worked with life rather than against it.

This change did not occur all at once.

Lifespans declined gradually.

Generation by generation, the effects of deterioration became more visible. What had been sustained began to shorten.

The shift reflects a process—not a sudden collapse.

The flood marks a clear turning point. After it, lifespans decrease more rapidly. This was not only a moment of judgment, but a transformation of the world itself.

The environment changed, and with it the conditions that had supported longer life. What had been preserved began to diminish more quickly.

Scripture also connects this period with increasing corruption. The condition of humanity affected more than behavior.

It influenced the direction of life as a whole.

As disorder increased, its effects extended beyond the individual. What had been sustained began to weaken—both within humanity and within the world they inhabited.

The long lifespans in Genesis are not anomalies.

They reflect a different stage of creation—one not yet fully deteriorated.

What is experienced now is not the original state, but what remains after decline has taken its course.

These early years point back to something lost.

They remind us that what is now considered normal was not always so.

Human life, as first created, carried strength and endurance that has since faded.

The record of those long lives is not only historical.

It reflects a world closer to what God intended.

Section 2: The "Aging Curve" After the Flood

Genesis records a clear shift in human lifespan after the flood. Before it, lives extended for centuries. After it, those years declined—generation by generation.

This pattern is not random.

It reflects change—both in the world itself and in the condition of humanity.

The flood marks a turning point. The environment that once supported long life was altered. What had been stable no longer functioned in the same way.

Conditions that once preserved life began to wear it down.

This would affect how the human body endures over time. What once sustained longevity was no longer present in the same form.

The decline that followed was gradual.

Lifespans did not suddenly fall to their present range.

Instead, they decreased across generations.

This reveals a process—not a single moment.

What had been strong became progressively weaker.

Scripture also connects this period with the ongoing effects of sin. What entered humanity did not remain isolated.

It continued to shape each generation that followed.

This influence was not only moral—it affected the condition of life itself.

What had once been resilient began to show fragility.

The change was both external and internal.

Shortened lifespans can be misunderstood as only judgment.

Scripture suggests something more.

Limiting time also limits the spread of corruption. In a world affected by sin, extended life would allow disorder to deepen unchecked.

A shorter span places a boundary on how far that influence can extend within a single life.

This shift also changed how life unfolds. No individual life stretched across centuries in the same way. Generations turned over more quickly, altering how history progressed.

Patterns of influence did not remain fixed as long.

The movement of time began to carry events forward differently.

What had once been prolonged became more transitional.

Within this change, a larger purpose is revealed. Shorter lifespans create a rhythm that moves history forward. They prepare the way for unfolding stages in God's plan—covenant, nations, and ultimately redemption.

What may appear as limitation is part of a larger direction.

Since that point, the general span of human life has remained relatively consistent. This stability reflects a lasting shift in both the world and humanity.

What was established after the flood continues—not as an isolated moment, but as an ongoing condition.

The decline in lifespan points beyond biology.

It reveals that the present world is not designed to be permanent.

Human life is limited—not to diminish its value, but to give it direction.

Time is not extended indefinitely.

It is given with purpose.

The aging curve is more than a record of decreasing years.

It reflects a changed world, the effects of corruption, and the boundaries of mercy.

What was reduced was not only lifespan—but the assumption that life in this world would continue without end.

Section 3: What Scripture Suggests About Longevity

The change in human lifespan is not presented as random. It follows a pattern that reflects both the condition of creation and the direction of God's work within it.

What appears as a simple decline in years carries deeper meaning when seen in context.

The long lifespans in Genesis point to a world not yet fully deteriorated. Even after the fall, creation retained much of its original strength.

The human body, the environment, and the condition of the world supported life in ways no longer present.

What is described in those early chapters is not exaggeration, but a reflection of a different state of creation—one closer to its beginning.

The flood marks a clear shift. After it, lifespans decline rapidly before settling into a consistent range.

This change reflects more than numbers.

It indicates that the conditions sustaining longer life had been altered.

What once supported endurance began to weaken—and that weakening became part of the human experience.

This decline reveals more than biology.

It reflects the continued unfolding of the fall.

As creation weakened, human life mirrored that condition. What had once been resilient became fragile. What had once been extended became limited.

The change is not isolated to the body—it is connected to the condition of the world.

At the same time, limitation carries purpose. Shortened lifespan is not only loss—it also functions as restraint.

In a world affected by sin, extended time would allow corruption to deepen.

A shorter span places a boundary on how far that influence can extend within a single life.

What appears restrictive also serves to contain what would otherwise continue unchecked.

This shift changes how life is understood. As time becomes limited, its significance becomes clearer.

It is no longer something to rely on indefinitely.

It becomes something to use with intention.

Human life is not designed to settle into permanence on earth—but to point beyond it.

Scripture moves the focus away from the length of life and toward its purpose.

Long life may be described as a blessing—but it is not the goal.

The greater promise is not extended years, but eternal life.

What was once experienced in part is brought into fullness through Christ.

Seen together, both early and later lifespans point beyond themselves. The longer years reflect what once was. The shorter years reflect the present condition.

Both direct attention toward something greater.

Human life is not defined by how long it lasts—but by what it is aligned with.

Longevity, then, is not simply a matter of years.

It reflects meaning.

It reveals a changed world, a humanity in decline, and a God who continues to move history toward its purpose.

The question is not how long life extends—but where it leads.

15

CREATION GROANS

Section 1: The Fall and the Fracture of Creation

The fall did not remain confined to humanity. It extended into creation itself. What began as separation from God became a disruption that reached into the order of the world.

The fracture was not symbolic—it altered how creation functions.

In the beginning, creation operated in full alignment with God. There was no resistance, no decay, no internal disorder. Everything moved in consistency with its design.

The natural world reflected the character of its Creator—ordered, stable, and whole.

When sin entered, that alignment was broken. The ground itself was affected. What once produced freely began to resist.

What once supported life now required effort.

This was not an isolated change, but a shift in the condition of creation as a whole.

Decay followed.

Death became part of the created order.

What had been sustained began to deteriorate.

Cycles of breakdown and renewal replaced what had once been continuous.

What is now observed in nature reflects this condition.

Stability was also altered. What had been consistent became less predictable. Patterns that once held began to shift.

The natural world no longer responded in the same way.

There is now resistance where there had been cooperation.

This extended to living creatures. The relationship between humanity and the rest of creation changed. What had once been ordered became shaped by survival.

Instinct replaced alignment.

Distance replaced what had been natural.

Scripture describes this as subjection to decay.

Creation is not holding its original state.

It is wearing down.

What exists now is not a return to what was, but the continuation of a condition that has already changed.

Paul describes this directly—creation groans.

This reflects tension, not metaphor.

There is strain within the natural world.

What is present does not match what was intended.

The visible condition carries the mark of disruption.

Creation mirrors humanity.

As humanity became fractured, so did the world it inhabits.

The outward instability reflects an inward break.

The two are connected.

Yet this condition is not final.

What has been affected will be restored.

The present disorder is not the end—it is part of a movement toward renewal.

Section 2: Natural Forces Within a Broken System

Destructive events in nature often raise the same question: where is God?

These moments may appear random, but Scripture frames them differently. They do not point to the loss of God's authority, but to the altered condition of creation.

Before the fall, creation did not operate in conflict with itself. There was no internal opposition within the natural world.

When sin entered, that order was disrupted. The ground was affected. Creation no longer functioned in full alignment.

Scripture describes this as creation groaning.

It reflects imbalance and strain.

The instability observed in nature is not isolated.

It is the expression of a world no longer ordered as it was.

Natural forces now operate within this condition. Patterns exist, but they are no longer fully stable.

What was once consistent now carries unpredictability.

Events that reshape environments and disrupt life reflect this broader reality.

This is not God introducing chaos.

It is creation functioning in a fractured state.

What has changed is not His rule, but the condition of what He governs.

God's authority remains intact.

Creation still responds to Him.

The instability of the system does not remove His control over it.

These moments also expose human limitation. They interrupt the assumption of control. What appears secure can shift. What seems stable can change.

This is not meant to produce fear, but clarity.

Within disruption, response emerges. People recognize what matters. Priorities shift. Compassion becomes visible.

This does not remove loss, but it reveals that even within brokenness, traces of what was intended remain.

This condition is not permanent.

Scripture points toward restoration.

What is disordered will be made whole.

What is unstable will be restored.

The present condition is transitional, not final.

These events are not evidence of God's absence.

They reveal a creation that has been affected and is awaiting renewal.

Section 3: Creation as a Continuous Witness

Creation continues to speak. Its condition has changed, but its purpose has not.

It still reveals the One who made it.

Scripture presents creation as a constant witness. It does not speak intermittently, but continually.

The natural world reflects something of God's nature.

It is not neutral—it carries meaning.

Even in a fallen state, creation retains order, structure, and beauty.

These are not accidental.

They point beyond themselves.

What is seen directs attention to its source.

There are also patterns within creation that repeat. Cycles of growth, rest, and renewal remain consistent.

These patterns are not only functional—they reflect design.

What unfolds outwardly often mirrors what occurs within.

At times, this witness becomes unmistakable.

What is usually observed quietly becomes overwhelming.

In those moments, human limitation is exposed. Control is revealed to be partial.

There are boundaries that cannot be overcome by human effort.

Creation reveals these limits.

It shows that life is not sustained by human control.

These limits serve a purpose.

They direct attention away from self-sufficiency and toward dependence.

Scripture also points to creation's future. Its current condition is not permanent.

What is marked by strain carries the expectation of restoration.

Creation is moving toward renewal.

This movement finds its meaning in Christ. What creation reflects is fulfilled in Him.

The order, the patterns, and the restoration all point to Him.

Seen together, creation is not disconnected from truth.

It reveals it.

The structure of the world, the limits within it, and its movement toward renewal all point beyond themselves.

Creation does not only inform.

It calls for response.

PART IV

THE PATH BACK
TO CLARITY

16

HEARING GOD CLEARLY

Section 1: The Unseen Is Primary

There is a dimension of reality that cannot be seen, yet it is more enduring than what is visible.

Scripture makes this clear: what is seen is temporary, while what is unseen remains.

This reverses how life is often interpreted.

What appears solid is not ultimate.

What cannot be seen sustains everything.

The visible world does not stand on its own.

It reflects what exists beyond it.

What is observed is not the source, but the result.

Interpreting life only through circumstances will always be incomplete.

What is seen does not explain what is happening.

This unseen reality is not distant.

It is present within ordinary life.

Influence, guidance, and resistance operate beneath the surface of daily experience.

The issue is not access, but attention.

What is unseen is often overlooked because focus remains fixed on what is visible.

Human beings were created with the capacity to recognize more than what can be measured.

Yet that capacity is often unused.

Attention becomes centered on what can be explained or controlled.

Over time, what is unseen becomes unfamiliar—and what is unfamiliar is dismissed.

Scripture calls for a different orientation. It does not deny what is visible, but it does not treat it as complete.

What appears outwardly often reflects something deeper.

Without this perspective, events are misread.

What is spiritual is reduced to what seems natural.

From the beginning, the pattern is consistent: what is unseen comes first, and what is seen follows.

Faith is not blind—it is the recognition of what exists before it becomes visible.

It responds to what is already real.

Jesus lived with this awareness. He did not react only to what was in front of Him. He discerned what was beneath it.

His clarity came from alignment with what was unseen, not dependence on circumstances.

Discernment begins with this shift.

It is not about seeing more, but recognizing what is already present.

Subtle awareness, quiet conviction, and inner clarity are not incidental.

They are indicators of something real.

The unseen is not secondary.

It is primary.

What is visible reflects it but does not define it.

When this becomes clear, interpretation changes.

What appears is no longer the final measure of what is true.

Section 2: The Distortion of Perception

The first battle is not external.

It is how reality is interpreted.

Spiritual blindness is not the absence of sight, but distortion.

What cannot be recognized cannot be resisted.

Perception becomes central.

Distortion develops gradually.

It does not require complete blindness.

Small shifts in interpretation are enough.

When perception changes, decisions follow—often without question.

Experience shapes this process. Pain, fear, and rejection influence how situations are understood.

What is neutral can begin to feel threatening.

What is true can become filtered.

Over time, these interpretations become familiar.

Familiarity is mistaken for accuracy.

Distraction weakens perception.

Attention determines clarity.

When attention is divided, awareness dulls.

What is subtle becomes difficult to recognize.

Truth does not disappear, but it becomes less noticeable.

Deception builds within this environment.

It rarely appears as something obviously false.

It aligns with existing assumptions.

Small distortions accumulate until what is misaligned feels normal.

What feels normal is rarely examined.

Cultural influence reinforces this.

It shapes what is accepted and what is ignored.

Over time, these patterns become internal.

Without correction, perception reflects what is common rather than what is true.

There is also resistance to clarity.

Confusion, pressure, and fatigue affect how reality is processed.

Clarity exposes what is hidden, and because of this, it is often opposed.

Pride makes distortion harder to detect.

When conclusions are held without question, correction becomes unlikely.

Certainty replaces discernment.

Yet certainty is not the same as clarity.

Restoration of perception does not come through effort alone.

It comes through alignment.

Truth must become the standard by which everything is interpreted.

As this happens, clarity returns gradually.

The issue is not increasing perception, but correcting it.

When perception is aligned with truth, it becomes stable.

It begins to guide, protect, and direct.

Section 3: Formation of Spiritual Clarity

Clarity is not immediate.

It is formed.

Those who discern accurately are shaped over time. What appears as insight is the result of development beneath the surface.

Scripture shows this pattern consistently. Those who saw clearly were prepared before they were recognized.

Their perception was not instant—it was formed.

What is visible in them reflects what was established within them first.

This formation begins with stillness.

When noise is reduced, attention becomes focused.

As attention focuses, awareness sharpens.

What was once overlooked becomes recognizable.

Stillness is not passive.

It creates alignment.

There are periods where what is seen does not match what is understood.

These moments create tension.

They require trust beyond appearance.

This is where perception deepens.

It moves from dependence on what is visible to confidence in what is true.

Discomfort often accompanies this process.

Familiar patterns begin to break down.

What once guided interpretation no longer holds.

This creates space for correction.

What feels unstable is often where clarity begins to develop.

Surrender is required.

Assumptions and expectations can distort perception if they remain unchallenged.

Letting them go allows truth to define what is seen.

Truth becomes the anchor.

Without it, interpretation shifts with circumstance.

Truth provides consistency.

It corrects what is inaccurate and stabilizes perception.

This process is guided.

The Spirit develops awareness that recognizes alignment.

This guidance is often subtle, but becomes clearer as it is followed.

What once required effort becomes more natural.

Discernment strengthens through repetition.

Patterns repeat, and recognition increases.

What was once unclear becomes familiar.

Clarity grows with use.

Perception is not developed for its own sake.

It exists to align life.

What is seen informs what is done.

Clarity directs action.

The goal is not to see more, but to see correctly.

When perception is aligned with truth, it becomes stable.

What begins as limited awareness becomes consistent understanding.

17

DISCERNING GOD'S VOICE

S ection 1: God Is Already Speaking
God is not silent.
He is continually communicating.

The issue is not whether He speaks, but whether His voice is recognized.

What often feels like absence is unfamiliarity.

What is present goes unnoticed when it is not understood.

From the beginning, Scripture reveals a God who initiates.

He speaks to create, direct, correct, and reveal.

His voice is not distant or occasional.

It is consistent.

He speaks because He desires to be known—not in theory, but in relationship.

His communication is not random.

It carries intention.

Hearing is not reserved for a few.

It is part of belonging to Him.

Jesus describes His people as those who recognize His voice.

This recognition does not begin fully formed.

It develops through familiarity.

What is heard repeatedly becomes easier to identify.

What was once uncertain becomes recognizable over time.

Clarity does not come from trying to make God speak more clearly.

It comes from learning how He already communicates.

Much of the struggle is shaped by expectation.

When His voice is limited to a specific form, it is often overlooked.

As understanding expands, recognition becomes more consistent.

What once seemed unclear begins to settle into pattern.

Scripture remains the primary anchor.

It establishes what is true, corrects what becomes misaligned, and stabilizes perception.

Without it, interpretation becomes unstable.

Other impressions may appear convincing, but they lack a fixed reference.

Scripture does not compete with other forms of communication.

It governs them.

God also communicates internally.

This often appears as clarity, conviction, or a steady sense of direction.

It does not demand attention or create pressure.

It aligns.

It carries consistency that does not fluctuate with emotion.

It remains steady even when circumstances shift.

What begins internally is often confirmed externally.

Through people, patterns, or repeated moments, what is forming becomes reinforced.

These confirmations do not create direction.

They clarify what is already present.

When internal and external align, recognition strengthens.

Not all communication comes through words.

Some moments are sensed rather than spoken.

A shift in awareness, a recurring impression, or quiet clarity can carry meaning.

These require attentiveness rather than analysis.

What is subtle is often missed when everything is approached through reasoning alone.

This recognition develops over time.

What is unfamiliar at first becomes easier to identify.

Patterns begin to emerge.

What once required effort begins to feel natural.

The voice does not change.

Recognition does.

God's voice is not limited to one method.

It is consistent in source, even when expression varies.

Understanding this removes confusion.

It allows listening to expand without losing stability.

God is already speaking.

The movement is not from silence to sound, but from unfamiliarity to recognition.

What once felt distant becomes consistent when attention aligns.

Section 2: What Interferes With Clarity

God's voice is not the only one present.

The issue is not availability, but interference.

Noise reshapes attention and gradually dulls awareness.

It does not need to be overwhelming to be effective.

It only needs to remain constant.

This noise builds through accumulation.

Activity fills time.

Internal thought fills space.

Emotional weight shapes interpretation.

External input keeps attention divided.

Each of these may seem manageable on its own, but together they create a condition where clarity becomes difficult to maintain.

Clarity rarely disappears suddenly.

It fades.

What was once noticeable becomes easy to overlook.

What once prompted reflection begins to pass without attention.

Over time, what is constant becomes normal.

What is normal is no longer questioned.

The result is not silence, but confusion.

God has not stopped speaking, but His voice becomes harder to distinguish.

Other influences begin to take precedence.

Emotion becomes louder.

External input becomes dominant.

Internal reasoning becomes constant.

What remains is a mixture that feels unclear.

As this continues, perception begins to shift.

Discernment weakens.

Decisions become more reactive than directed.

Familiar patterns begin to replace clarity.

What is known becomes less influential than what is immediate.

Clarity requires space.

Attention cannot remain divided and still recognize what is subtle.

Moments must exist where noise is reduced—both internally and externally.

When that space is created, awareness begins to settle.

In that settling, separation begins to occur.

What was previously blended together becomes distinct.

What is true begins to stand apart from what competes with it.

Clarity is not created in that moment.

It becomes visible.

This process is not neutral.

There is resistance to clarity.

Anything that overwhelms attention or distorts perception works against alignment.

Recognizing this changes how noise is approached.

It is no longer incidental.

It must be addressed.

As interference is reduced, awareness returns.

What was unclear begins to take shape.

Direction becomes easier to recognize.

This does not happen because God begins to speak more, but because what He is already communicating is no longer obscured.

Clarity does not need to be forced.

It emerges when what competes with it is removed.

The voice being sought has not been absent.

It has been present beneath the interference.

Section 3: Living With Clear Discernment

Hearing clearly is not accidental.

It is formed over time.

Clarity develops where space is created and attention is aligned.

What feels difficult becomes consistent when the conditions for awareness are present.

Environment plays a significant role.

Just as physical hearing depends on reduced noise, spiritual clarity depends on inner condition.

When distractions are reduced, awareness increases.

When attention is gathered, perception sharpens.

Certain patterns support this development.

Silence quiets what competes for attention.

Solitude removes distraction and gathers focus.

Consistency builds familiarity.

These are not techniques to control an outcome.

They are conditions that allow clarity to emerge.

Space must be made intentionally.

When life is filled without pause, perception becomes crowded.

Not everything that fills that space is wrong, but much of it competes for attention.

Reducing what is unnecessary creates room for clarity to surface.

Posture also shapes perception.

A teachable heart remains open rather than fixed.

Assumptions are not held rigidly.

Correction is not resisted.

This posture allows truth to reshape understanding rather than being filtered through what is already assumed.

Recognition requires response.

What is perceived must be followed.

When it is, awareness sharpens.

When it is ignored, sensitivity diminishes.

Over time, this creates a pattern.

Clarity increases where there is response, and confusion increases where there is resistance.

Discernment develops through repetition.

Patterns repeat in different forms, and recognition becomes more immediate.

What is aligned remains steady.

What produces confusion becomes easier to identify.

This distinction strengthens over time.

With consistency, clarity stabilizes.

What once required effort becomes natural.

What once felt uncertain becomes steady.

Awareness is no longer occasional.

It becomes part of how life is lived.

The goal is not to hear more, but to hear correctly.

Clarity leads to alignment, and alignment produces confidence.

Direction is no longer forced.

It is recognized.

God's voice is not distant.

It becomes familiar where attention is aligned and response is consistent.

What once felt difficult settles into clarity—not because something new has been added, but because what was already present is now being recognized.

18

THE RENEWED MIND

Section I: The Mind as the Battleground
The primary conflict is not external.
It takes place within the mind.

Thought determines direction.

It is the lens through which everything is interpreted—God, people, circumstances, and purpose.

When that lens is distorted, everything that follows is affected.

Scripture does not stop at salvation.

It points to transformation, and that transformation begins with the renewal of the mind.

This is not driven by effort alone, but by a shift in how reality is understood.

Life follows thought.

What is believed consistently shapes perception, and perception directs response.

The mind becomes the battleground.

External conditions do not need to change if interpretation is influenced.

Subtle ideas, persistent fears, and repeated assumptions can shape an entire life without altering circumstances.

What is believed internally begins to govern what is lived externally.

There is no neutral state.

The mind is always being formed.

It is shaped either by what surrounds it or by what is true.

One reflects what is visible.

The other reflects what God reveals.

This formation is continuous.

What is repeated becomes established, and what is established begins to feel natural.

Tension develops when internal alignment has not caught up with spiritual reality.

It is possible to experience change while still thinking in old patterns.

Truth may be known but not applied.

Faith may be present, but fear remains active.

This creates conflict—not because truth is absent, but because perception is not yet aligned.

The mind assigns meaning to everything experienced.

Situations are not only lived through—they are interpreted.

What appears negative may carry purpose.

What feels uncertain may be part of formation.

Without renewal, meaning is often misassigned.

Repeated thoughts become structures.

These patterns feel stable, even when not rooted in truth.

Built from assumptions, fear, and repetition, they begin to guide interpretation automatically.

What is inaccurate can feel normal simply because it is familiar.

Renewal requires intentional replacement.

Old patterns do not disappear on their own.

They must be exchanged for what is true.

As truth is applied consistently, perspective begins to shift.

This change is not theoretical—it becomes practical.

A renewed mind does not ignore reality.

It interprets it correctly.

It recognizes what is not immediately visible and remains steady where reaction would normally take over.

This steadiness is clarity, not denial.

Everything that follows in life begins here.

When the mind is renewed, direction changes.

When direction changes, life begins to align.

Section 2: Two Ways of Thinking

If the mind is the battleground, perspective determines the outcome.

There are two ways of interpreting life—one shaped by what is seen, and one shaped by what is true.

Every thought moves in one of these directions.

One way of thinking is formed by environment.

It develops through culture, experience, and limitation.

It reacts to what appears.

The other is formed by alignment with truth.

It interprets what is seen in light of what is not immediately visible.

This difference becomes clear in how lack is understood.

A natural mindset focuses on what is missing and responds with control or anxiety.

A renewed mind begins from what is already secure.

It trusts provision even when not yet visible.

The situation may not change, but the response does.

Pressure is also interpreted differently.

Fear magnifies uncertainty and weakens stability.

A renewed mind remains anchored.

It does not deny pressure but does not allow it to define reality.

It responds with steadiness.

Timing reveals the same contrast.

Delay can be interpreted as failure or absence.

A renewed perspective recognizes formation.

What appears slow may be developing something not yet seen.

The issue is not the delay, but how it is understood.

Obstacles are often misread.

What appears to block progress may be shaping direction.

What feels like interruption may carry purpose.

A natural perspective resists disruption.

A renewed mind pauses and discerns.

Identity follows the same pattern.

One approach builds identity through performance, approval, and outcome.

It shifts constantly.

A renewed mind begins from what has already been established.

Identity is received, not constructed.

This creates stability.

Emotion also influences perception.

Feelings are real, but they are not final.

When they become the primary guide, interpretation becomes unstable.

A renewed mind does not dismiss emotion but does not allow it to define truth.

Circumstances are no longer the final reference point.

A natural mindset depends on what can be measured.

Confidence rises and falls with conditions.

A renewed mind remains anchored beyond what is visible.

Meaning is not determined by appearance alone.

This shift is not optimism.

It is alignment.

A renewed mind does not deny reality—it interprets it correctly.

It sees beyond what is immediate and remains steady where others react.

Transformation begins with perspective.

When thinking changes, direction follows.

When direction changes, life aligns.

Section 3: The Process of Renewal

Renewal is not a moment.

It is a process that develops over time.

It requires consistency.

What is repeated begins to reshape how thoughts are formed.

Change begins when truth moves from being known to being internal.

What is held, revisited, and applied begins to influence thinking.

Repetition replaces what was previously assumed.

Old patterns remain until they are replaced.

What is inaccurate must be released, and what is true must take its place.

This exchange reshapes internal dialogue.

Reactions begin to slow, awareness increases, and new patterns begin to form.

Repetition is essential.

What is practiced becomes familiar.

What becomes familiar begins to feel natural.

Response changes—not because effort increases, but because alignment becomes consistent.

Attention directs this process.

What is focused on consistently becomes the framework for interpretation.

When attention is intentional, clarity increases.

When it is scattered, confusion remains.

Expression reinforces alignment.

What is spoken strengthens what is believed.

Agreement with truth reduces internal resistance.

Over time, what is expressed and what is believed align.

Identity anchors this process.

When identity is unstable, interpretation shifts.

When identity is established, perception becomes steady.

Seeing correctly begins with understanding who you are.

Not every thought should be accepted.

Some must be examined and released.

Renewal requires bringing thoughts into alignment with truth rather than allowing them to remain unchallenged.

This development is gradual.

It unfolds through consistent alignment.

What once required effort becomes natural.

What once felt unclear becomes steady.
The goal is not to think more, but to think correctly.
When perspective changes, direction follows.
A renewed mind is cultivated, not forced.
What was once distant becomes familiar.
What required effort becomes consistent.
Clarity becomes the way life is lived.

19

SPIRITUAL AUTHORITY

Section 1: Authority Begins With Position
Spiritual authority is often misunderstood.
It is not defined by volume, personality, or force.
It is not control or intensity.

Authority is the right to stand in what God has established and to represent what He has declared.

This authority does not begin with ability.

It begins with identity.

It is not earned—it is given.

The moment a person belongs to Christ, their position changes.

They are placed within what has already been established.

This becomes the starting point.

Authority flows from position, not effort.

It is not something that must be reached or created.

It already exists.

When this is misunderstood, confidence becomes unstable because it depends on performance.

When it is understood, clarity settles because it rests on what does not change.

Authority is not self-generated.

It does not come from personal strength or intensity.

It functions through alignment.

It carries weight because it is connected to a greater source.

For this reason, it does not need to prove itself.

It remains steady.

This shapes the posture of authority.

It is not aggressive or reactive.

It is settled.

It does not seek attention or display.

It carries a quiet confidence that does not depend on expression.

Its strength is in alignment.

Before authority is expressed, it is formed through submission.

It does not begin with action but with surrender.

Life is brought into alignment first.

From that alignment, authority begins to operate.

Without this foundation, expression becomes inconsistent.

Authority is revealed through obedience.

It is not occasional, but consistent.

Each aligned response reinforces what has already been established.

Over time, this creates stability.

Authority is carried through how life is lived.

It is not carried alone.

Authority is supported by what God has already established.

What is lived out does not depend on personal strength.

Recognizing this removes pressure and replaces it with confidence.

At its core, authority is not about becoming powerful.

It is about understanding where you stand.

When position is clear, expression becomes natural.

There is no need to strive for what has already been given.

Section 2: Authority Functions Through Alignment

Understanding authority is foundational.

Learning how it functions brings clarity.

Authority is not emotional or reactive.

It operates within order and becomes effective through alignment.

It does not function everywhere in the same way.

It operates within what has been entrusted.

There are areas of responsibility, influence, and calling where it is active.

When alignment is maintained within those areas, clarity increases.

When it is not, effectiveness diminishes.

Authority follows placement, not ambition.

When placement is clear, direction becomes defined.

Response becomes intentional rather than reactive.

What once felt uncertain begins to settle into clarity.

Authority is connected to purpose.

It is not given for display.

It exists to establish what aligns with God's will and to confront what does not.

It builds, protects, and restores order.

It becomes most visible where there is resistance.

Opposition does not indicate failure.

It often reveals that something is active.

When alignment is present, it creates tension with what opposes it.

This tension is part of the process.

Authority does not react to resistance.

It remains steady.

It does not depend on emotion.

It responds from alignment.

Pressure does not produce confusion.

It sharpens clarity.

Authority does not operate randomly.

It functions through consistent alignment with truth.

As alignment deepens, expression becomes more effective.

Authority is not developed through declaration, but through consistency.

Expression follows alignment.

What is spoken reflects what is already established within.

When alignment is present, words carry weight.

When it is absent, they do not.

Authority influences environments.

Clarity increases.

Confusion diminishes.

Stability replaces reaction.

What is carried internally begins to shape what is experienced externally.

This is because authority does not originate within the individual.

It flows from a greater source.

It remains steady because that source does not change.

Authority is not about striving.

It is about alignment.

When alignment is present, authority functions naturally.

Section 3: Walking in Quiet, Confident Authority

Authority becomes real when it is lived—not in isolated moments, but in consistency.

It is not something turned on when needed.

It is something carried.

It is not expressed through intensity.

It is revealed through stability.

Authority flows from alignment.

When the inner life is steady, expression becomes clear.

This is why true authority often appears quiet.

Confidence does not come from self.

It develops through awareness—an awareness that you are not standing alone.

As this awareness grows, fear loses influence.

Pressure becomes less defining.

Clarity becomes consistent.

Authority is formed through humility.

Humility keeps authority aligned with its source.

It removes the need to prove or defend.

When humility is present, authority remains clear.

When it is absent, it becomes distorted.

Discernment guides authority.

It is not constant action, but accurate response.

There are moments to speak and moments to remain still—moments to engage and moments to step back.

Discernment determines the difference.

Authority strengthens through consistency.

It is not built in isolated expressions, but through daily alignment.

What is practiced becomes natural.

Stability develops over time.

The inner life remains central.

What is carried within determines what is expressed.

When the inner life is clear, authority flows.

When it is not, clarity weakens.

Authority cannot be separated from the condition of the heart.

It responds from truth rather than reacting to pressure.

Circumstances may shift, but response remains steady.

What is carried does not change with what surrounds it.

At its core, authority is not something to achieve.

It is something to recognize and walk in.

When alignment is present, expression becomes natural.

Quiet, confident authority is steady, grounded, and consistent.

It is not forced.

It is lived.

20

WALKING IN THE LIGHT

Section I: Revelation Must Become Expression
Revelation is one of the clearest ways God makes Himself known.

It is not meant to remain information.

It carries direction.

What is revealed is meant to be followed.

Without response, revelation remains incomplete.

Throughout Scripture, revelation leads to movement—not simply because something has been understood, but because something has been acted upon.

It does not exist to be observed.

It calls for response.

It moves from awareness into action.

Revelation carries responsibility.

What is seen must be lived.

When it is not, a separation forms between what is known and how life is shaped.

Truth was never meant to remain theoretical.

It is given so it can take form in daily life.

Growth is not measured by how much is understood, but by what is practiced.

Knowledge can remain in the mind without producing change.

Transformation becomes visible only when understanding begins to shape how life is lived.

When revelation is not applied, clarity weakens.

What once felt sharp becomes less defined.

This is not because truth has changed, but because it has not been followed.

What is not acted on begins to lose influence.

It is possible to continue receiving insight without experiencing transformation.

This creates imbalance.

Learning increases, but change does not follow.

The appearance of growth can remain while the substance is missing.

Over time, this disconnect becomes harder to recognize because familiarity replaces awareness.

Revelation is meant to move beyond awareness.

It is intended to shape patterns, influence decisions, and become part of how life is lived.

When this happens, understanding becomes formation.

What was once insight begins to take root and produce change.

This process develops through consistency.

What is acted upon becomes established.

What is established becomes natural.

What once required effort becomes the way you think, respond, and move through life.

What is established begins to shape identity.

Change becomes steady rather than temporary.

It is no longer something you return to—it becomes something you live from.

At its core, revelation is not complete until it is expressed.

What is given is meant to produce fruit.

When it remains unexpressed, it remains unfinished.

Revelation is not the end.

It is the beginning of a life shaped by what has been seen.

Section 2: A Life That Reflects Truth

Revelation is not meant to stop with you.

It is meant to be seen through you.

When truth takes form in a life, it becomes visible.

What is lived becomes something others can recognize, even if they cannot fully explain it.

Growth moves from understanding into embodiment.

What is known begins to shape how life is lived.

This creates consistency.

A life shaped by truth becomes steady, and that steadiness becomes its own form of communication.

Influence begins here—not through effort, but through what is consistently carried.

What is repeated becomes recognizable.

What is recognizable begins to carry weight beyond words.

People are drawn not to explanation alone, but to evidence.

A life that reflects alignment creates clarity for others.

It shows what is possible without needing to prove it.

This kind of influence does not force attention.

It holds it.

What is visible is shaped by what is internal.

Character, integrity, and honesty are not separate from truth.

They are expressions of alignment.

When the inner life is steady, the outer life becomes reliable.

This influence is not built through perfection, but through authenticity.

A life that allows growth to be seen creates trust.

It does not hide process or struggle, but it does not center them.

It reflects change as it happens.

Love remains central.

Truth without love can be resisted.

Love shapes how truth is carried.

It gives clarity a form that can be received rather than rejected.

Without it, what is true can feel distant.

With it, it becomes transformative.

Consistency reinforces everything.

Patterns form through steady alignment that becomes visible.

Influence is not built in isolated moments, but through what is lived consistently.

What is lived does not remain limited to the present.

It carries forward.

The way truth is lived today becomes something others can build upon tomorrow.

Influence extends beyond immediate outcomes into places that may never be seen.

A life shaped by truth does not draw attention to itself.

It points beyond itself.

Its purpose is not to gather attention, but to provide direction.

When this remains clear, influence stays healthy.

Revelation becomes powerful when it is lived.

What is lived can be seen.

What is seen can be followed.

Section 3: Daily Alignment That Becomes a Way of Life

Revelation is not proven in moments, but in choices.

It is not defined by what is felt in an encounter, but by what is lived afterward.

What is revealed finds its meaning in daily decisions.

Transformation becomes visible through consistency.

It shows up in small choices that are often unnoticed.

What is chosen repeatedly becomes direction, and that direction shapes the course of a life.

These small decisions carry more weight than they appear.

What seems insignificant in the moment begins to accumulate.

Patterns form.

Those patterns begin to define how life is lived.

As this develops, life begins to take order.

Time is approached with intention.

Focus becomes clearer.

What once distracted begins to lose its hold.

What once competed for attention becomes easier to release.

The inner life also changes.

Reactions slow.

Awareness increases.

Emotions no longer determine direction.

They are understood within a larger framework where truth remains the reference point.

Boundaries begin to take shape.

Not everything is allowed to remain.

Not every opportunity is pursued.

What is recognized as important begins to guide what is embraced and what is released.

Identity remains central.

When identity is clear, decisions stabilize.

There is less need to respond to pressure, comparison, or expectation.

What is known internally begins to shape what is chosen externally.

Obedience becomes simpler.

What is understood begins to guide what is done.

This is not driven by pressure, but by alignment.

Alignment forms rhythm, and rhythm becomes a way of life.

Revelation moves from insight into practice.

What begins as awareness becomes expression.

What is expressed consistently becomes pattern.

What becomes pattern begins to feel natural.

This process unfolds step by step.

It is not about carrying everything at once, but walking in what is known.

As each step is followed, clarity increases.

What was once distant begins to come into view.

Over time, something shifts.

The distance between knowing and living begins to close.

What was once separate becomes unified.

Life is no longer divided between understanding and action.

The result is not effort, but alignment.

Not pressure, but clarity.

Not striving, but consistency.

Revelation is not the destination.

It is the beginning of a life shaped by what God has made known.

And when that life is lived, it becomes visible—not as a moment, but as a pattern; not as an event, but as a way of being.

What began as revelation becomes light.

And that light is no longer something you see—it becomes the way you walk.

FINAL BLESSING AND PRAYER

A Prayer for Eyes That See and a Heart That Trusts

May the Lord bless you with the gift this book has sought to awaken—not the comfort of having all the answers, but the confidence of walking with the One who does.

May your eyes be opened to the unseen, your spirit attuned to the whisper of God, and your mind renewed by truth that is higher, deeper, and more beautiful than anything this world can teach.

May every place of confusion be replaced with clarity. May every place of fear be overcome by faith. May every place of uncertainty be met with divine assurance.

May every step you take from this day forward be guided by revelation, not reaction... by peace, not pressure... by discernment, not distraction.

I pray that the Holy Spirit Himself would illuminate your path, guard your perception, and steady your heart in every season.

May He teach you to hear the Shepherd's voice above every noise, to walk in quiet authority, and to trust God in the silent places where He is forming you the most.

May you become a person of revelation—one who walks in

wisdom, sees with spiritual clarity, and carries the light of Christ into a world desperate for truth.

And now, may the grace of the Lord Jesus Christ, the love of God the Father, and the fellowship of the Holy Spirit rest upon you, fill you, and lead you into all truth... now and forever.

Amen.

ACKNOWLEDGMENTS

First and foremost, I give thanks to my Lord and Savior, Jesus Christ. He breathed life into these pages and walked with me through every valley and mountain. Without His grace, wisdom, and sustaining power, there would be no story to tell and no testimony to share.

To my children—Tania, Javier, David, Iliana, Jason, and Keila: thank you for being my strength and my reason. You have carried burdens few will ever understand, and your quiet resilience has been a light in my darkest seasons. Your love, even when unspoken, has lifted me more than you know.

To my granddaughter Yamalis: thank you for your tenderness, courage, and the joy you bring to our family. Watching you step into motherhood has filled me with renewed hope and deep gratitude for the legacy God is building through you.

To my beloved wife, Cheryl Marie: thank you for your unwavering love, patient spirit, and steadfast faith. You have stood beside me in seasons of sorrow and celebration. Your quiet strength, sacrificial love, and faithful prayers have anchored both my life and my ministry.

To my co-pastor and dear friend, Pastor Héctor Matías: thank you for walking this road of ministry with me. Your integrity, loyalty, and devotion to God's people have been a gift. To you and your family, I extend my deepest gratitude for your extraordinary generosity in helping make the editing and formatting of this book possible. When resources were limited, your kindness became a lifeline. You reminded me that God still sends people to lift our hands when the journey grows heavy.

To Minister Yolanda Rosado: your humility, steadfastness, and servant's heart continue to inspire all who know you. Thank you for your prayers, wisdom, and unwavering support in every season.

To the Rock of Salvation Church family: you are living proof that dry bones can rise again. Thank you for believing in the vision God placed in my heart. Your encouragement, faith, and love have carried this message far beyond our sanctuary walls.

And finally, to every reader: thank you. If you have journeyed with me to this final page, you are now part of my story. My prayer is that these words lead you from religion into relationship, from tradition into truth, and from brokenness into the fullness of life found only in Christ.

He alone is the Author of this testimony—and the One who walked beside me every step of the way.

ABOUT THE AUTHOR

Pastor Jose R. Perez is a pastor, communicator, and spiritual mentor with more than four decades of ministry experience. Known for his clarity, compassion, and prophetic insight, he has devoted his life to helping believers hear God's voice, navigate seasons of uncertainty, and walk confidently in the light of revelation. His teaching combines deep biblical understanding with a commitment to making spiritual truth accessible, practical, and transformational for everyday life.

Pastor Perez leads Rock of Salvation Church in Worcester, Massachusetts—the first Hispanic evangelical church in the city, founded by his parents, Reverend Jose Perez and Reverend Ramona Perez. Born in Puerto Rico and raised between two cultures, his life is a testimony of redemption: from addiction, grief, and family fragmentation to restoration, purpose, and Spirit-led leadership.

Over the years, he has served his community in many roles—pastor, nonprofit director, union organizer, mentor, and advocate—always with a heart for justice, healing, and spiritual renewal. His ministry is marked by a commitment to revival, reconciliation, and the unfiltered truth of Scripture, free from religious distortion or cultural compromise.

Carrying forward the legacy entrusted to him by his father, Pastor Perez continues to proclaim a message of hope, repentance, and spiritual awakening to a generation searching for more than tradition—they are searching for truth.

In *The Gift of Not Knowing: How Letting Go Opens the Way to Deeper Faith*, Pastor Perez invites readers into a deeper, more authentic walk with Christ—one shaped not by legalism or performance, but by grace, surrender, and the power of the Holy Spirit. He writes especially for the wounded, the weary, and for all who are ready to rise again.

THE GIFT OF NOT KNOWING SERIES

CONNECT WITH THE AUTHOR

If this book has blessed, challenged, or strengthened you, Pastor Jose R. Perez would love to stay connected with you.

You can follow his ministry, access new teachings, and receive updates on future books through the links below.

Website

www.PastorJosePerez.com

Teachings, events, updates, and resources

Email

Info@pastorjoseperez.com

For prayer requests, ministry invitations, or testimonies

Social Media

Instagram: https://www.instagram.com/pastorjoserperez/

TikTok: https://www.tiktok.com/@pastorjoserperez

YouTube: https://www.youtube.com/@PastorJoseRPerez

Facebook: https://www.facebook.com/jose.r.perez.3363

Books & Resources

All books by Pastor Perez—including upcoming releases in *The Gift of Not Knowing* series—are available through:

Amazon Author Page:

www.amazon.com/author/pastorjoseperez

If this book has impacted your life, consider leaving a review on Amazon. Your words help others discover this message and allow it to reach more people.

Thank you for helping spread the gospel through this work.